SEASONS OF LIFE™
Designs for Living Summer's Journey

Editor *Carol Shea*

Plans Editor *Tina Leyden*

Art Director *Sheri Potter*

Graphic Designers *Yen Gutowski*
Brooke Pfutzenreuter

Illustrator *Heather Bettinger*

Rendering Colorization *Alva Louden*

Rendering Illustrators *Shawn Doherty*
Silvia Boyd
Perry Gauthier
George McDonald, dec.

Technical Adviser *Jody Marker*

Managing Editor *Kevin Blair*

Circulation Manager *Priscilla Ivey*

Publisher *Dennis Brozak*

Associate Publisher *Linda Reimer*

SEASONS OF LIFE™
Designs for Living Summer's Journey

is published by:
Design Basics Publications
11112 John Galt Blvd., Omaha, NE 68137
Web – www.designbasics.com
Email – info@designbasics.com

Chief Executive Officer *Dennis Brozak*

President *Linda Reimer*

Director of Marketing *Kevin Blair*

Business Development *Paul Foresman*

Controller *Janie Murnane*

Cover Photo: Plan #28B-2248 Laverton
As seen on page 34

Builder: Dennis Smit Construction

Library of Congress Number: 98-70602
ISBN: 1-892150-01-8

Living **S**ummer's Journey

With its rapid growing season that lasts just a few months out of the year, it's quite comparable to the lifestage of those who are busily raising their families... And as families grow and to "move up" becomes a priority, one activity parents won't want to rush is their selection of a home in which they'll raise their children.

Summer. It is a time that bustles with activity, as blossoms turn to fruit before our very eyes. With its rapid growing season that lasts just a few months out of the year, it's quite comparable to the lifestage of those who are busily raising their families. In the fullness of their summer season, today's families spend their time attending soccer games and dropping kids off to dance, while trying to remember to call a babysitter for the spouse's company golf outing next Saturday. Though all the rushing around makes many long for simplicity, most wouldn't trade this time in their life for anything. And as families grow and to "move up" becomes a priority, one activity parents won't want to rush is their selection of a home in which they'll raise their children.

◆ Emotional Investment ◆

Today's move-up buyers span the gamut from the Baby Boomers to Generation X. As much research indicates the decisions they make, especially in housing, are a result of their impressions and attitudes formed early in life. Because Baby Boomers, for the most part, grew up with Mom at home, they were raised in relatively secure, safe environments. And now that they are parents themselves, they crave that same sense of security they remember growing up. They are not, however, looking for their parents' homes. Their need for nostalgia has transcended into a desire for informality and convenience in a home. While in the 80s they may have been interested in "keeping up with the Joneses," this group of buyers is more interested in homes that makes sense and complement their daily lifestyle. Today's move-up families are more concerned about the emotional – not financial investment in their homes. Homes are no longer just a place to park your car and sleep at night. They are returning to society as the center of family life.

◆ Family Focus ◆

Without a doubt, accommodating childrens' needs is the most important priority for today's move-up families. According to authors J. Walker Smith and Ann Clurman, 6_ percent of today's Boomer parents say they express themselves through raising their children. Another 47 percent say they spend time with their kids to relax. This is perhaps true because fewer and fewer children have the luxury of having a parent stay home to raise them. In housing, that translates to big entertainment rooms, large backyards and open kitchens that can accommodate a whole family wanting to spend time together.

◆ Separation ◆   Yet, as much as move-up buyers need homes with places to interact, they need places to get away, if need be. With the varied activities of today's family, some separation is necessary whether it be for homework, office work or simply time to oneself. This means the home must have separate areas, such as bedrooms for each child, master suites with a quiet sitting area, or even a den that's away from it all.

◆ Entertainment "Centers" ◆   Baby Boomers were the first generation to grow up watching television as a daily activity. Their counterparts, Generation X, have doubled their viewing time in front of the tube. Consequently, family rooms and entertainment centers are important lifestyle features. User-friendly, home automation systems are also popular with today's move-up buyer. The countless remote controls scattered across dens and family rooms are testament to the need for an organized system that makes sense. These "smart" homes appeal to their busy lifestyle, especially for the technologically savvy Generation X family.

◆ Home Offices ◆   As the family focus continues, and as computer technology continually advances, more and more adults are choosing to take advantage of the opportunity to work out of their homes. Because of this, home offices are one of the biggest requests from today's move-up buyer. Having a separate, dedicated space to work, not only makes working out of the home more efficient, it also helps keep work space separate from the family living area.

◆ Flexible Rooms ◆   While different generational characteristics come into play when choosing a home, so also does the varied make up of today's families. Today's move-up buyer may be a single-parent, a married couple with children from previous marriages or an extended family household. Not only does home have to reflect a family's desires, it also has to coincide with its varied structure. A key component in home design and a home's resale value is the adaptability of its rooms. Today's move-up families need homes with "flex" areas that may easily be used for storage, later finished for a home office and eventually used as a guest suite by the home's next buyer.

Summer's Journey ◆   Seasons Of Life, Designs for Living Summer's Journey embraces the needs and desires of today's move-up buyer. The following 100 designs are especially tailored to the varied make-up of modern families, providing a wide variety of square footages and choices. No matter what stage of life, home should be an enjoyable daily experience. It seems this should especially be true for growing families. It's fitting to keep in mind that while their choices in housing reflect their own generational characteristics, these homes will, in turn, play a part in shaping a new generation. Their choices will lay the foundation for the exciting journey ahead. ◆

If Our House Was Human

My house has become the victim of a family that's outgrown and outpaced it. We've grown and changed so quickly, we've hardly had time to notice the lopsided state it's in. Our home is like a jacket that pulls at our shoulders and is short in the sleeves. Now that I've actually taken some time to look, I'm surprised we didn't notice it earlier. Our house simply doesn't fit us anymore.

Walk through my house on a typical day and you'll see me studying on the dining room table. You'll find my daughter surfing the net on our home computer located in, of all places, the living room. You'll also see our treadmill in the living room, next to some toy space aliens strewn out underfoot. And all throughout the home you'll hear the vibrating drone of a bass guitar as my son thumbs his way through his latest song in the basement.

So much has changed since the day we first laid eyes on our current home. I grew up in the southern part of town, and wanted to stay in that vicinity. After walking through a slew of homes that were either out of our price range or too run down, there it was: a multi-level with an eat-in kitchen, dining room, two living areas and three bedrooms. It was perfect, we thought. There were plenty of places for our children to spread their toys out and play. The bedrooms were close by and there was a big backyard for a swing set. But as our family grew and changed, our home remained, as homes do, the same place we moved into. And so we have a treadmill sitting where a couch should be.

But as our family grew and changed, our home remained, as homes do, the same place we moved into. And so we have a treadmill sitting where a couch should be.

If our house was human, however, and could have grown and changed as we have, it would have anticipated our needs and adapted our living room into an office, for example. It would have changed our basement into a "rec room" for the kids and an exercise area for my husband and I. It may have opted to expand our master suite to include an area where we could have placed a couple of chairs to relax. It would have anticipated my daughter's doll collection and built shelves into her room. It would have foreseen my son's budding musical talent and

Paterson

#28B-1380 Price Code B19

Main Floor:	1421 Sq. Ft.
Second Floor:	578 Sq. Ft.
Total Square Feet:	1999 Sq. Ft.

cont'd on next page

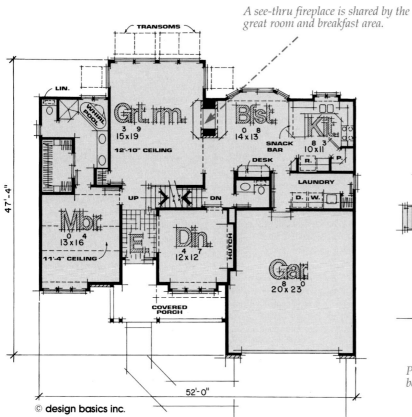

A see-thru fireplace is shared by the great room and breakfast area.

TRANSOMS

LIN.

Grt. rm.
3   9
15x19

12'-10" CEILING

Bfst.
0   8
14x13

SNACK
BAR

Kt.
8   3
10x11

WHIRL
POOL

DESK

LAUNDRY

R.   P.

D.   W.

UP   DN

Mbr.
0   4
13x16

11'-4" CEILING

Dn.
4   7
12x12

HUTCH

Gar.
8   0
20x23

COVERED
PORCH

47'-4"

52'-0"

© design basics inc.

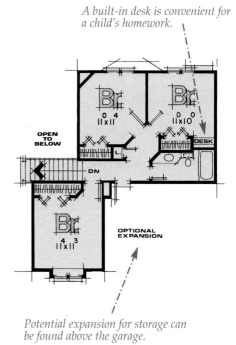

A built-in desk is convenient for a child's homework.

Br.
0   4
11x11

Br.
0   0
11x10

DESK

OPEN
TO
BELOW

L.

DN

Br.
4   3
11x11

OPTIONAL
EXPANSION

Potential expansion for storage can be found above the garage.

Sinclair

Total Square Feet: 1911 Sq. Ft.

#28B-1748 Price Code B19

A second bedroom is flexible as den or bedroom.

A built-in entertainment center makes the hearth room a welcome area for relaxation.

An angled see-thru fireplace makes a great showpiece in the great room.

ENT. CENTER

TRANS.

Hrth.
10⁰x14⁰

Bfst.
10⁰x10³

Mbr
13⁰ x 15⁵

9'-4" CEILING

OPTIONAL DEN

Br
12⁰x11²

Grt. rm.
16³ x 22⁸

SNACK BAR

Kit.
13⁰x10⁶

P.

WHIRLPOOL

SKYLIGHT

10'-0" CEILING

SKYLIGHT

DN

W.

Br
12⁰x11³

Dn
12⁰ x 13⁰

12'-0" CLG

W.
D.

LIN.

COVERED STOOP

Gar
21⁴ x 21⁸

58'-0"

56'-0"

© design basics inc.

double or triple insulated hi room. It woul have noticed m daughter's new found love o baking and ex panded its kit chen counter to accommodate the two of u and our accumulating appli ances. It would have notice my kids' attraction to the inter net and telephone and woul have built in extra jacks an phone lines. It would hav understood video game system and found an alcove in its fam ly room for an extra TV. Ou house would have realized th necessity of separation betwee our bedroom and the children bedrooms. It would have grea ly expanded its closets an moved the laundry room nea our bedrooms.

But my home is n human. And while it couldn anticipate our needs, neithe could we foresee our curre muddled situation when u moved in. But then again, wh would have thought of th need for separate compute space? Back when we boug our first home, compute filled whole rooms.

Who'd have thought about the placement

◊ cont'd on next page

❖ SEASONS OF LIFE ~The SUMMER YEARS ❖

Hallmark

#28B-3535 Price Code B25

Total Square Feet: 2504 Sq. Ft.

NOTE: 9 ft. main level walls

The openness between the gathering room, kitchen and breakfast area will make it the hub of everyday family activity

A screened-in porch, privately located off the breakfast area, would be the perfect place to enjoy a meal outdoors.

This home's four-stall garage accommodates the teenagers' vehicles

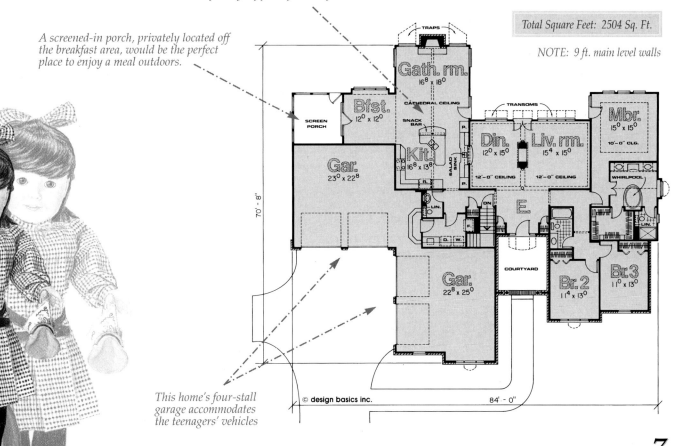

© design basics inc.

Main Floor: 1412 Sq. Ft.
Second Floor: 425 Sq. Ft.
Total Square Feet: 1837 Sq. Ft.

Pine Ridge

#28B-8096 Price Code A18

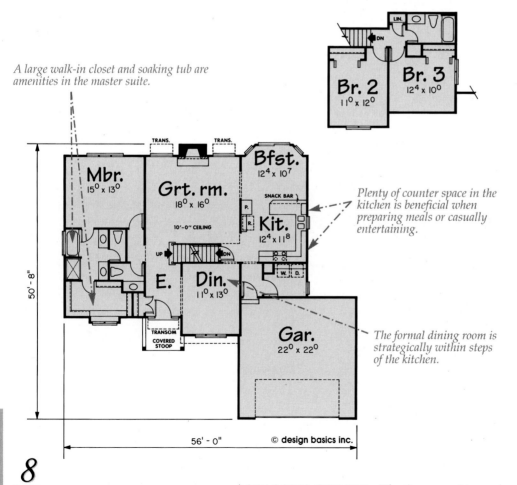

A large walk-in closet and soaking tub are amenities in the master suite.

Plenty of counter space in the kitchen is beneficial when preparing meals or casually entertaining.

The formal dining room is strategically within steps of the kitchen.

of the laundry room? Our parents considered themselves lucky to "have" a laundry room. And my husband and I washed our clothes in a laundromat before moving in.

Who'd have thought about the possibility of a young musician "plugging in" each night to the chagrin of the rest of the household?

Who'd have thought I'd return to college and need space to study?

Certainly not the two of us who'd lived 10 years in a tiny one bedroom house. A mere 800 square feet, our first home had one bathroom and one phone jack location that allowed calls from any room in the house. It was only after we'd had our first son, a.k.a. Eddie Van Halen, that we felt the need to move. And when we set foot in our current home, we felt as if we were kings.

Time to move, yet again? Who'd have thought? Certainly not us. And certainly not – even if it were human – our current home. ◆

◆ *SEASONS OF LIFE ~The SUMMER YEARS* ◆

Kirkwood

#28B-4646 Price Code B18

Main Floor: 1285 Sq. Ft.
Second Floor: 568 Sq. Ft.
Total Square Feet: 1853 Sq. Ft.

Walk-in closets in two secondary bedrooms provide more space for storage.

SLOPED CEILING

OPEN TO GRT.RM.

16'-5" CEILING

Br.4
11^0 x 10^0

DN

L.

Br.3
11^0 x 10^0

Br.2
11^0 x 10^0

Extra storage in the garage provides a place for tools and lawn equipment.

An open railing offers a unique vista into the great room.

Grt.Rm.
15^4 x 18^0

Sto.

W. D.

Din.
11^0 x 11^4

SNACK BAR

DN

UP

Gar.
22^0 x 20^8

Kit.
11^0 x 12^0

P. R.

E.

COVERED PORCH

Mbr.
14^0 x 14^0

42'-8"

© design basics inc.

59'-8"

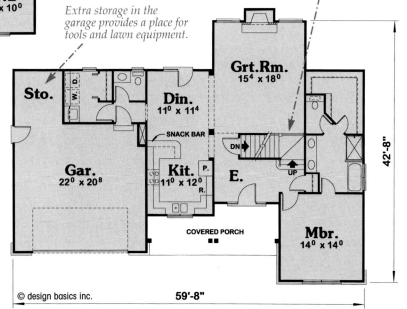

Linden

#28B-2638 Price Code B21

> Main Floor: 1082 Sq. Ft.
> Second Floor: 1021 Sq. Ft.
> Total Square Feet: 2103 Sq. Ft.

An indented doorway into the walk-in closet of the master suite is the perfect place for a three-way mirror.

A T-shaped staircase streamlines traffic flow to the second floor.

The parlor is located just inside the entry and makes a great private area to relax.

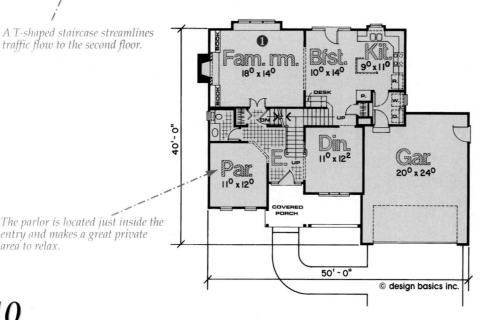

© design basics inc.

One of our favorite things to do as a family on a weekend night is to rent movies. It's inexpensive, and it's also a way for all of us to be together. Because of this, we've invested a lot of money in our entertainment unit. Its many components almost "require" purchasing an entertainment center. But we are reluctant to do this, since they eat up so much space in a room. What I really wish is that we had a home with an entertainment center built into our TV room...

SOLUTION

In the Linden's family room (❶, at left and interior view), built-in shelves on either side of the fireplace perfectly adapt to the electronic equipment of your choice. A designated media room on the second floor of the Durand (❷, at right) provides a place for just the kids or the whole family to get together.

Durand

#28B-2671 Price Code B30

Main Floor: 1923 Sq. Ft.
Second Floor: 1106 Sq. Ft.
Total Square Feet: 3029 Sq. Ft.

A wet bar/servery located in the dining room is a great asset when entertaining guests.

An exquisite master bath showcases French doors that reveal an oval whirlpool and his and her vanities.

Bedroom 2 offers its own 3/4 bath and walk-in closet. Because of this, it works well as a guest suite.

Media rm.
16⁰x17⁸

Br. 4
13⁰x11⁰

Br. 2
12⁰x12⁰

Br. 3
12⁰x12⁰

OPEN TO BELOW

DESK ENT. CENTER DESK

UP DN

Bfst.
13⁰x13⁸

Grt. rm.
16⁰x20⁰

Mbr.
13⁰x16⁰

Kit.
13⁰x12⁰

Gar.
22⁸x28⁸

Din.
13⁰x14⁴

Par.
12⁰x14⁴

WET BAR

E.

STOOP

47'-4"

64'-0"

© design basics inc.

Paisley

#28B-2618
Price Code B21

ABOVE LEFT: Elegant French doors open to the living room, cradled with a set of bayed windows.

ABOVE RIGHT: A view into the family room shows off its warm fireplace and connection to the living room.

LEFT: This welcoming kitchen shows off its island cooktop and sun-filled breakfast area.

BUILT BY: **UNIQUE HOMES**
EXTERIOR PHOTO BY: **DESIGN BASICS INC.**
INTERIOR PHOTOS BY: **PAUL GATES**

The home in these photographs may be altered from the original plan.

Main Floor: 1093 Sq. Ft.
Second Floor: 1038 Sq. Ft.
Total Square Feet: 2131 Sq. Ft.

Extra storage space in the garage is an added benefit for home improvement projects.

French doors expand the living room and family room for large gatherings.

His and her compartments organize the walk-in closet in the master suite.

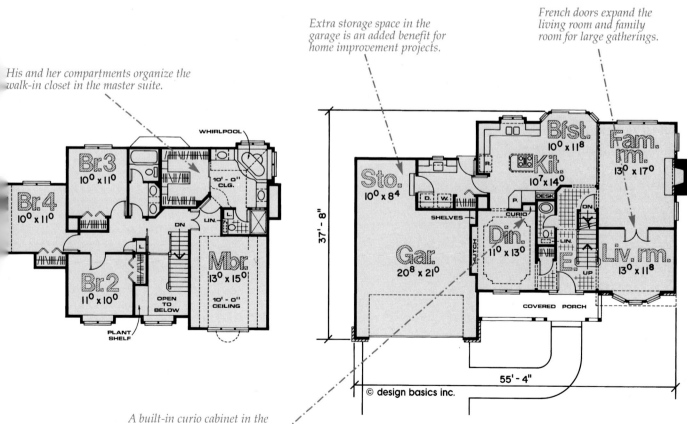

WHIRLPOOL

Br.3
10⁰ x 11⁰

Br.4
10⁰ x 11⁰

10' - 0"
CLG.

DN

LIN.

Mbr.
13⁰ x 15⁰

Br.2
11⁰ x 10⁰

OPEN
TO
BELOW

10' - 0"
CEILING

PLANT
SHELF

Sto.
10⁰ x 8⁴

SHELVES

Gar.
20⁸ x 21⁰

37' - 8"

Bfst.
10⁰ x 11⁸

Kit.
10⁷ x 14⁰

Fam.
rm.
13⁰ x 17⁰

Din.
11⁰ x 13⁰

CURIO

DESK

DN

UP

Liv. rm.
13⁰ x 11⁸

COVERED PORCH

55' - 4"

© design basics inc.

A built-in curio cabinet in the dining room provides a place for crystal and china.

SITUATION

Through the years, our family has grown and changed drastically. We've gone from needing a nursery, to needing a play area for the kids, to needing a place for our home computer. I can only imagine the needs we'll have as we grow older. If there's one thing our current house lacks, its the ability to change along with us. In our next home, we definitely need rooms that can adapt to our ever-changing needs. . .

SOLUTION

One of the biggest benefits of the Bentley Woods (❶, at right) is its exceptionally large bonus room located on the second floor. This area, with its quaint dormers, could easily be finished off to serve a variety of uses. The Attleboro offers a fifth bedroom on the main floor (❷, at far right) that, because of its location, doesn't have to be used as a bedroom and can easily suit the individual needs of today's families.

Bentley Woods

#28B-8082 Price Code A19

Main Floor: 945 Sq. Ft.
Second Floor: 1007 Sq. Ft.
Total Square Feet: 1952 Sq. Ft.

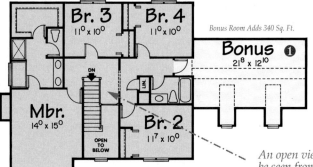

Br. 3
11⁰ x 10⁰

Br. 4
11⁰ x 10⁰

Bonus Room Adds 340 Sq. Ft.

Bonus ❶
21⁸ x 12¹⁰

Mbr.
14⁰ x 15⁰

DN

OPEN TO BELOW

LIN.

Br. 2
11⁷ x 10⁰

An open view of the two-story entry can be seen from the second-floor landing.

The kitchen is thoughtfully located within close proximity to both the breakfast area and formal dining room.

The back covered porch on this home is a great place to get away for a moment of seclusion.

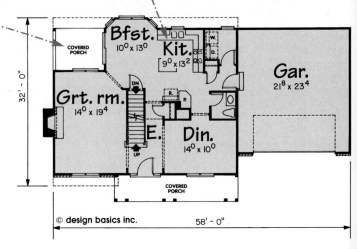

COVERED PORCH

Bfst.
10⁰ x 13⁰

Kit.
9⁰ x 13²

W.
D.

Gar.
21⁸ x 23⁴

Grt. rm.
14⁰ x 19⁴

DN

E.

Din.
14⁰ x 10⁰

UP

32' - 0"

© design basics inc.

58' - 0"

COVERED PORCH

Attleboro

#28B-5083 Price Code B27

Main Floor: 1582 Sq. Ft.
Second Floor: 1170 Sq. Ft.
Total Square Feet: 2752 Sq. Ft.

NOTE: 9 ft. main level walls

A walk-in pantry in the kitchen offers plenty of storage for food and kitchen equipment.

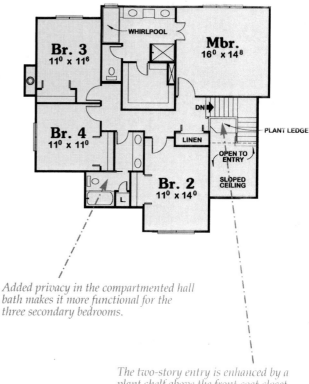

Added privacy in the compartmented hall bath makes it more functional for the three secondary bedrooms.

The two-story entry is enhanced by a plant shelf above the front coat closet.

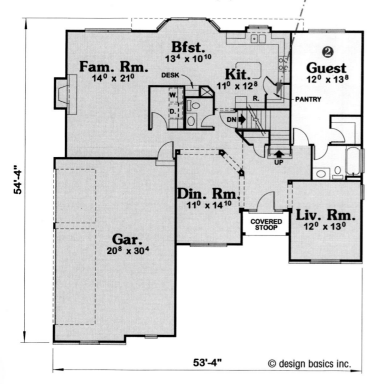

© design basics inc.

STORAGE . . .

For all our worldly possessions, we invariably need adequate and organized storage. While it might be for a functional item, usually it's for rolls of unruly Christmas wrap or scores of old photos and family heirlooms. To meet the needs of today's families and all of their "stuff," the following plans provide plenty of storage space.

FUTURE FLEX SPACE

Main Floor:	910 Sq. Ft.
Second Floor:	775 Sq. Ft.
Total Square Feet:	1685 Sq. Ft.

Adams Creek
#28B-8105 Price Code A16

The great room can expand into the dining room for more space and is open to the entry.

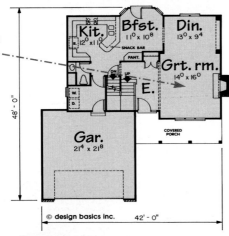

BOUNTIFUL BONUS ROOM

Main Floor:	1824 Sq. Ft.
Second Floor:	1580 Sq. Ft.
Total Square Feet:	3404 Sq. Ft.

Harrison
#28B-3174 Price Code B34

A private den located to the front of the home has a spectacular spider-beamed ceiling, transom windows and lovely double doors.

The 3-car garage has a corner storage closet, perfect for sporting equipment or household tools.

A U-shaped staircase leads to a second floor with a striking view of the entry.

Unfinished Bonus Room Adds 479 Square Feet

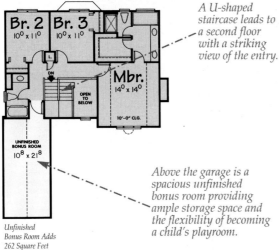

Above the garage is a spacious unfinished bonus room providing ample storage space and the flexibility of becoming a child's playroom.

Unfinished Bonus Room Adds 262 Square Feet

An unfinished bonus room above the garage provides excellent storage space and has the possibility for future expansion.

SEASONS OF LIFE ~The Summer Year

SPECIALIZED STORAGE

Main Floor: 1008 Sq. Ft.
Second Floor: 1136 Sq. Ft.
Total Square Feet: 2144 Sq. Ft.

Caldera

#28B-4952 Price Code B21

The spacious kitchen has abundant counter and cupboard space.

The bayed great room opens to the dining room for comfortable entertaining and family gatherings.

A handy storage space in the rear of the master suite's large walk-in closet is ideal for its expansion or built-in dressers.

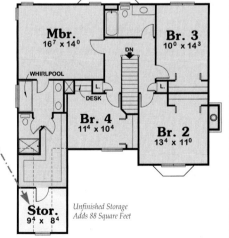

Unfinished Storage Adds 88 Square Feet

PRACTICAL EQUIPMENT SPACE

Main Floor: 1392 Sq. Ft.
Second Floor: 1153 Sq. Ft.
Total Square Feet: 2545 Sq. Ft.

Morrison

#28B-2229 Price Code B25

Extra storage is offered in the garage and is large enough for bicycles and lawn equipment.

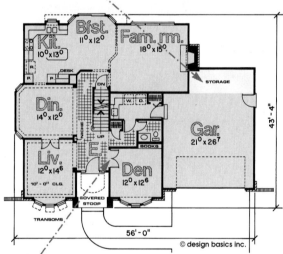

Elegant double doors lead to a secluded den complete with a bayed window and built-in bookshelf.

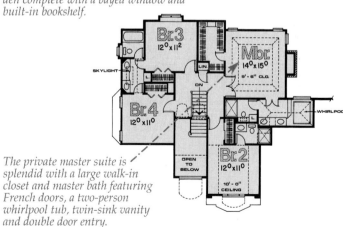

The private master suite is splendid with a large walk-in closet and master bath featuring French doors, a two-person whirlpool tub, twin-sink vanity and double door entry.

SENSIBLE WORKBENCH PLACE

Main Floor: 1303 Sq. Ft.	
Second Floor: 1084 Sq. Ft.	
Total Square Feet: 2387 Sq. Ft.	

Kendall

#28B-1553 Price Code B23

GREAT GARDEN CENTER

Main Floor: 1113 Sq. Ft.	
Second Floor: 965 Sq. Ft.	
Total Square Feet: 2078 Sq. Ft.	

Bristol

#28B-1870 Price Code B20

A salad sink and counter space doubles as a servery for the formal dining room.

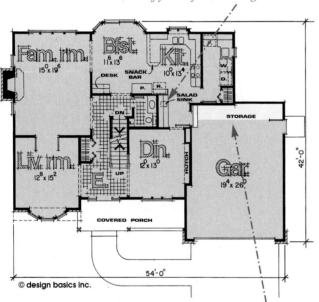

A sunken gathering room is open to the kitchen via an open railing.

© design basics inc.

Ample storage for a workbench is located in the garage.

The garage has its own storage area, suitable for a lawn and garden center.

© design basics inc.

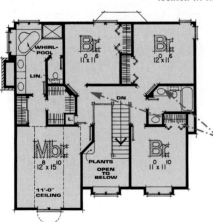

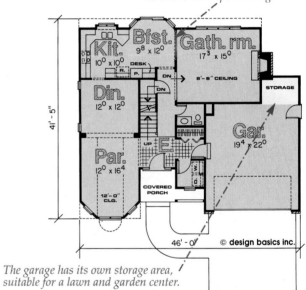

Interesting angles add design character and visual intrigue to the upstairs bedrooms.

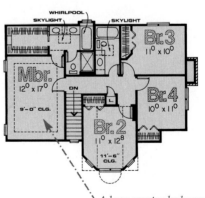

A long master bedroom has room for a couple of chairs.

❖*SEASONS OF LIFE ~The SUMMER YEARS*

EXPANSIVE FUTURE ROOM

Main Floor: 1179 Sq. Ft.
Second Floor: 1019 Sq. Ft.
Total Square Feet: 2198 Sq. Ft.

Stratman
#28B-3588 Price Code B21

...ing to the breakfast area and great room for entertaining conve-
...e, the efficient kitchen has an island counter and two lazy Susans.

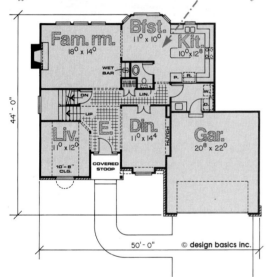

Window seats in two secondary bedrooms provide quiet areas for kids to study and read.

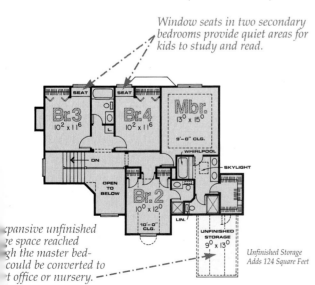

...pansive unfinished
...e space reached
...gh the master bed-
...could be converted to
...t office or nursery.

Unfinished Storage Adds 124 Square Feet

GREAT GARAGE ALCOVE

Main Floor: 1032 Sq. Ft.
Second Floor: 743 Sq. Ft.
Total Square Feet: 1775 Sq. Ft.

Juniper
#28B-2308 Price Code B17

The secluded family room expands comfortably into the breakfast and kitchen area.

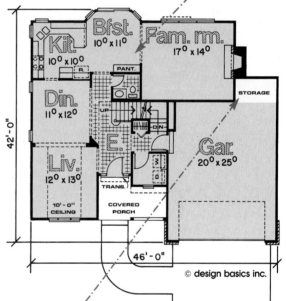

The garage includes a practical area for a workbench or storage.

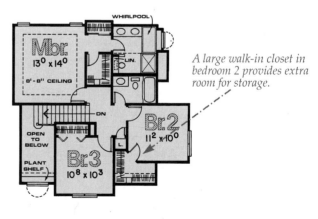

A large walk-in closet in bedroom 2 provides extra room for storage.

BUILT-IN MEDIA SHELVES . . . Catering

to today's families, built-in media centers provide efficient storage for stereos, televisions and stacks of compact discs and videos. As a result, the placement and design of media centers are very important. The following plans demonstrate the advantages of having built-in media shelves.

PAMPERING MASTER SUITE

| Main Floor: 1000 Sq. Ft. |
| Second Floor: 1345 Sq. Ft. |
| Total Square Feet: 2345 Sq. Ft. |

Franklin
#28B-2316   Price Code B23

The living room expands the family room through a set of elegant French doors.

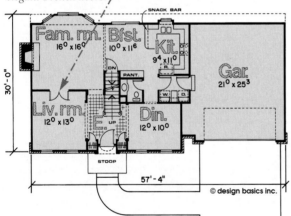

© design basics inc.

The lavish master suite is a perfect place to unwind with a built-in entertainment center, private sitting room and pampering master bath.

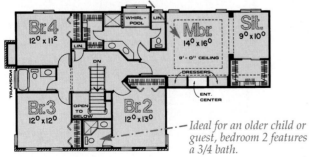

Ideal for an older child or guest, bedroom 2 features a 3/4 bath.

EVER-WELCOME ENTERTAINMENT CENTER

| Main Floor: 1923 Sq. Ft. |
| Second Floor: 1852 Sq. Ft. |
| Total Square Feet: 3775 Sq. Ft. |

Corinth
#28B-2332   Price Code B37

Helping accommodate a home entertainment center are built-in bookcases in the large family room.

A private, screened-in porch is a great place for quiet time alone.

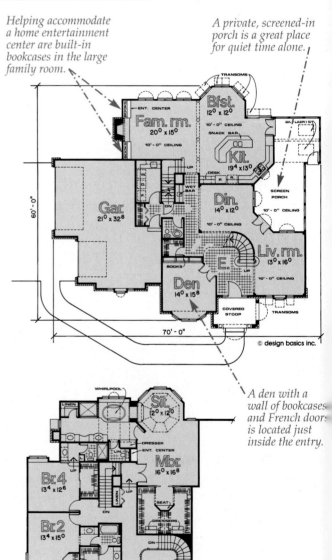

© design basics inc.

A den with a wall of bookcases and French doors is located just inside the entry.

SENSIBLE STEREO ACCOMMODATION

Main Floor: 1062 Sq. Ft.
Second Floor: 1023 Sq. Ft.
Total Square Feet: 2085 Sq. Ft.

Yorke

#28B-2217 Price Code B20

MADE FOR MOVIES

Main Floor: 1366 Sq. Ft.
Second Floor: 1278 Sq. Ft.
Total Square Feet: 2644 Sq. Ft.

Jennings

#28B-3246 Price Code B26

A bayed window, entertainment center and see-thru fireplace complement the family room.

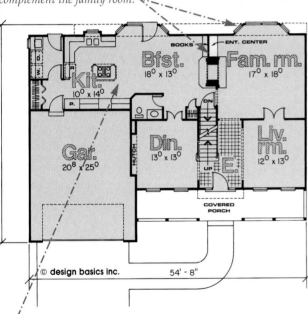

The kitchen openly shares space with the warm hearth room and breakfast area.

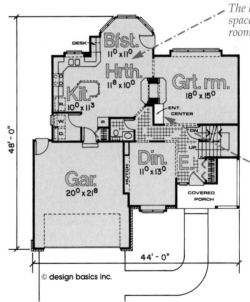

The great room's built-in entertainment center is perfect for the family TV and stereo equipment.

A spacious kitchen has plenty of room for the whole family.

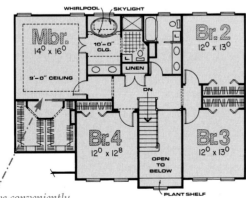

A dressing alcove conveniently accompanies the master suite's large walk-in closet.

His and her vanities in the large master bath provide separate areas for getting ready.

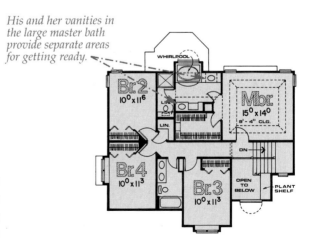

BENEFICIAL BOOKSHELVES

Main Floor:	1082 Sq. Ft.
Second Floor:	869 Sq. Ft.
Total Square Feet:	1951 Sq. Ft.

Cyprus
#28B-2648 Price Code B19

Bookshelves in the family room can easily be adapted to accommodate the family entertainment system.

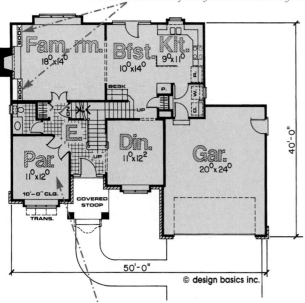

© design basics inc.

Whether used as an office, library or formal living area, the secluded parlor will be a sought-after location in the home.

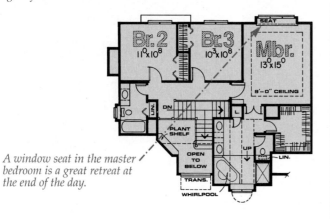

A window seat in the master bedroom is a great retreat at the end of the day.

MARVELOUS MEDIA CENTER

Main Floor:	1415 Sq. Ft.
Second Floor:	1274 Sq. Ft.
Total Square Feet:	2689 Sq. Ft.

Leawood
#28B-2779 Price Code B26

An open family room welcomes large groups with its built-in media center.

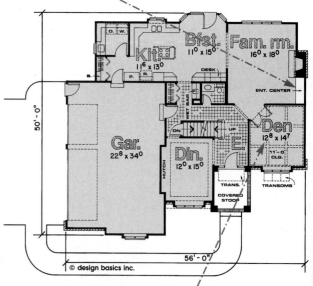

© design basics inc.

A handsome den with double doors features a spider-beamed ceiling and stately transom windows.

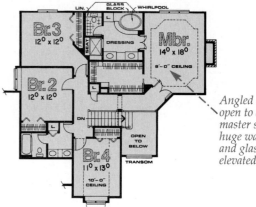

Angled double doors open to a secluded master suite with a huge walk-in closet and glass block over elevated whirlpool tu

✦ SEASONS OF LIFE ~The SUMMER YEARS

HANDY VIDEO CENTER

Main Floor:	1268 Sq. Ft.
Second Floor:	1075 Sq. Ft.
Total Square Feet:	2343 Sq. Ft.

Stanton
#28B-2414 Price Code B23

A see-thru fireplace, entertainment center and bookcase will be favorites in the volume family room.

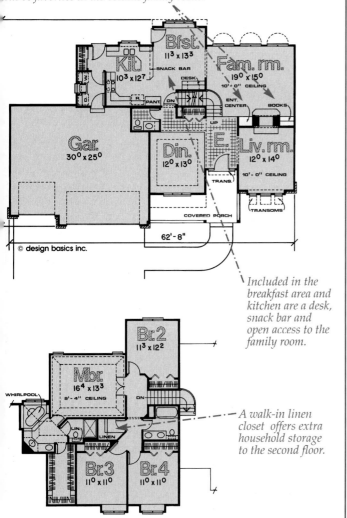

© design basics inc.

62' - 8"

Included in the breakfast area and kitchen are a desk, snack bar and open access to the family room.

A walk-in linen closet offers extra household storage to the second floor.

ADAPTABLE BOOKSHELVES

Main Floor:	884 Sq. Ft.
Second Floor:	848 Sq. Ft.
Total Square Feet:	1732 Sq. Ft.

Jefferson
#28B-2890 Price Code B17

Off the entry is the formal living room, featuring a fireplace between two bookcases that can be easily converted to entertainment centers if desired.

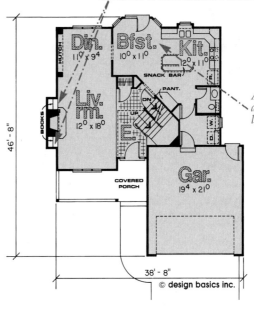

A bayed breakfast area adds spaciousness to a large island kitchen.

© design basics inc.

46' - 8"

38' - 8"

A quaint plant shelf is located mid-way up the U-shaped stairway.

My High Performance "Dream Home"

Everyone like me had a "dream car" and mine was the American Motors AMX. I was able to purchase a new 1974, medium metallic green model when I was 15 years old.

While many things fascinated me growing up, there were two things that unduly occupied my days and nights.

The first of these was my fascination with cars. You could say I was a "motorhead." I loved everything about them – their style, performance and make-up. Everyone like me had a "dream car" and mine was the American Motors AMX. I was able to purchase a new 1974, medium metallic green model when I was 15 years old. Having saved up enough money for half of its cost, my parents footed the rest of its $3,500 price tag. While in my possession, I added all the features to make it a truly sweet ride – a high-performance cam shaft, turbo charger and intake manifold, side pipes, fat tires, glass pack mufflers, shift kit, high stall torque converter, new rear end gears, new headers, a racing carburetor and two-tone fur lining to

Prairie

#28B-2285   Price Code B21

Main Floor: 1505 Sq. Ft.
Second Floor: 610 Sq. Ft.
Total Square Feet: 2115 Sq. Ft.

Br.3 11³ x 12⁰

Br.2 12⁴ x 11¹

Br.4 10⁸ x 12⁵ 10'-0" CLG.

OPEN TO BELOW

PLANT SHELF

A cathedral ceiling brings a sense of grandeur to the great room.

The kitchen is within steps of the formal dining room for easy service.

Grt. rm. 15³ x 22⁰ CATHEDRAL CEILING

Mbr. 13⁰ x 16⁰ 10'-0" CLG.

Bfst. 11⁴ x 14⁰

Kit. 9⁰ x 14⁰ SNACK BAR

Din. 14⁰ x 11⁵

Gar. 30⁷ x 22⁷

COVERED PORCH

WHIRL-POOL

TRANSOMS   TRAPS   TRANSOMS

52'-0"

64'-0"

© design basics inc.

Sloped ceilings bring a unique flair to this pampering master bath.

the dashboard and seats. It was beautiful.

All the attention my car received helped bring to life my long-standing dream of becoming an auto mechanic. I thought it would be the perfect job: seven days a week of fixing up Chevys, Fords and Mopars. I could hardly wait to see myself with creased hands and slate blue overalls, permanently blackened with the grease and grime of my trade. I could see my future – and the smoking tires of my jacked up AMX led the way.

The second of my obsessions was with football. The Green Bay Packers were (and still are) my team. And if I could have chosen to see myself as anyone, it would have been Bart Starr. Perhaps it's because I was watching as Starr lead the Packers to the first two Superbowl titles. My sing-song delivery of a tormenting "Na Na Na-Na Na" still rings sweetly in my head as I remember the Packers annihilation of my brother's team, the Oakland Raiders, in Superbowl II. In my dreams – or at least in the football tosses with my dad – I was Bart Starr, throwing tight spiraling passes with the effortless talent of a professional. When I was coerced into being the "tack-

cont'd on next page

Jordan Oaks

#28B-8035 Price Code A20

Main Floor: 1399 Sq. Ft.
Second Floor: 617 Sq. Ft.
Total Square Feet: 2016 Sq. Ft.

Unfinished Storage Adds 386 Sq. Ft.

Tall windows in the family room and bayed windows in the breakfast area bring in an abundance of natural light.

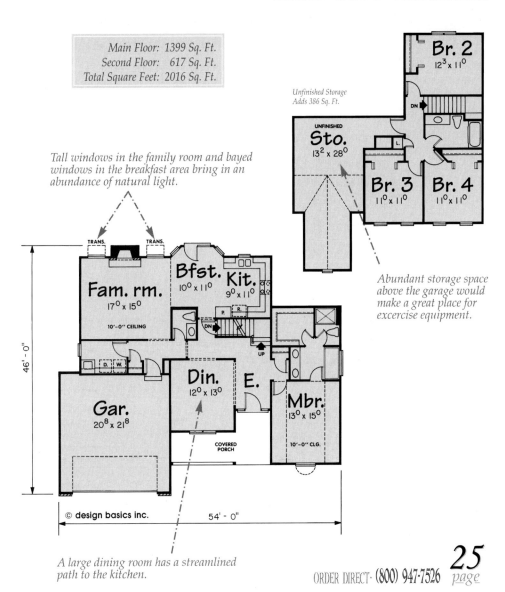

Abundant storage space above the garage would make a great place for excercise equipment.

A large dining room has a streamlined path to the kitchen.

Seville

#28B-2212 Price Code B17

Total Square Feet: 1735 Sq. Ft.

An island counter helps organize the kitchen.

The openness between the dining and great rooms is beneficial when hosting large groups.

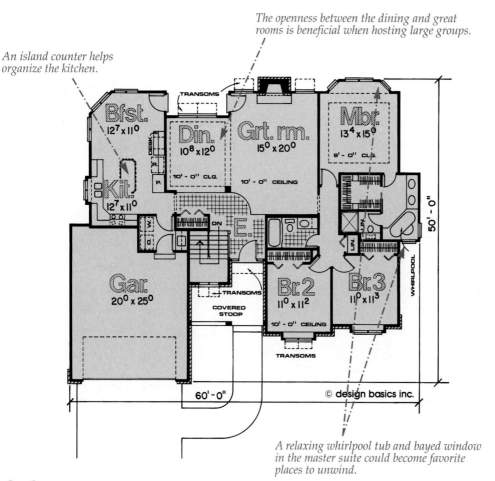

Bfst.
12⁷ x 11⁰

Din.
10⁸ x 12⁰
10' - 0" CLG.

Grt. rm.
15⁰ x 20⁰
10' - 0" CEILING

Mbr.
13⁴ x 15⁰
9' - 0" CLG.

Kit.
12⁷ x 11⁰

TRANSOMS

Gar.
20⁰ x 25⁰

Br. 2
11⁰ x 11²
10' - 0" CEILING

Br. 3
11⁰ x 11³

WHIRLPOOL

COVERED STOOP

TRANSOMS

TRANSOMS

50' - 0"

60' - 0"

© design basics inc.

A relaxing whirlpool tub and bayed window in the master suite could become favorite places to unwind.

♦ SEASONS OF LIFE ~ The SUMMER YEARS ♦

The Green Bay Packers were (and still are) my team. And if I could have chosen to see myself as anyone, it would have been Bart Starr.

ling dummy" for my older brother and his football friends, I was Bart Starr dodging the defensive linemen. Finishing my English essay, I was Bart Starr signing autographs. And reading it in front of the whole 4th grade class, I was Bart Starr worshiped by adoring fans.

But, alas, none of this was to be. After trying my hand in accounting, I ended up with a Marketing degree. I have since gotten married and, along with my wife, had four children. And even though I enjoy my job, there's no sense of freedom or rebellion that seems to surround the aura of an auto mechanic. There's nothing larger-than-life about my job like that of Bart Starr. Where's the romance in projecting the ROI on potential marketing projects? I have to wonder, as I drain the oil pan in our minivan, what life would've held, had I followed my dreams.

Would there be a mortgage? Would there be wrestling matches in the living room with my sons? Would there be hot dogs roasted over open

cont'd on next page

Castelar

#28B-2656 Price Code B25

Main Floor: 1362 Sq. Ft.
Second Floor: 1223 Sq. Ft.
Total Square Feet: 2585 Sq. Ft.

NOTE: 9 ft. main level walls

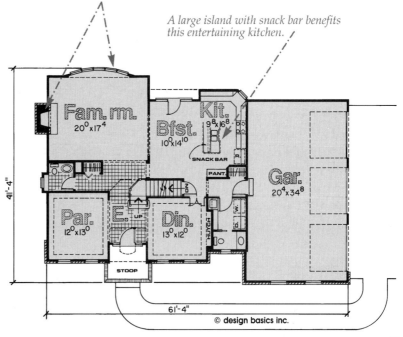

Walk-in closets in bedrooms 2 and 3 offer the potential for toy storage.

Bowed windows and a fireplace bring beauty to this large family room.

A large island with snack bar benefits this entertaining kitchen.

© design basics inc.

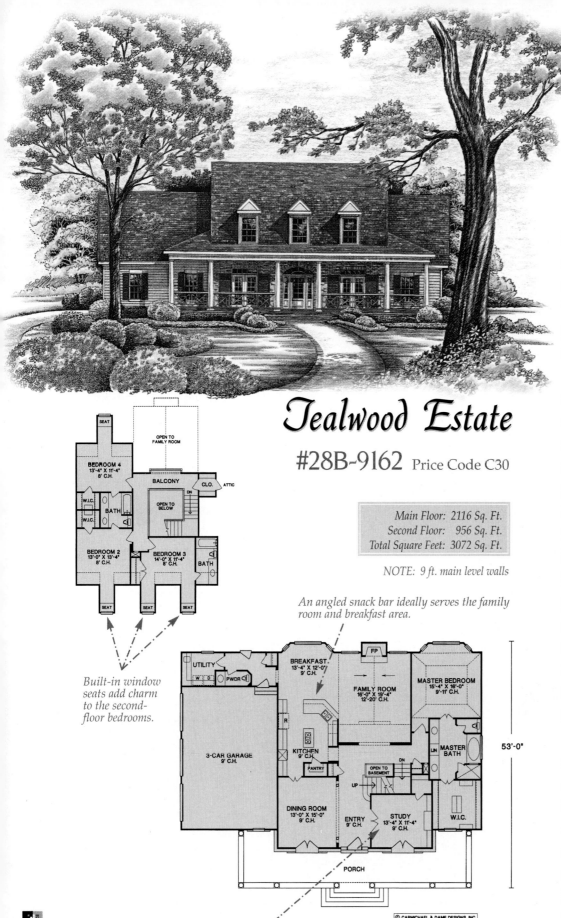

Tealwood Estate

#28B-9162 Price Code C30

Main Floor: 2116 Sq. Ft.
Second Floor: 956 Sq. Ft.
Total Square Feet: 3072 Sq. Ft.

NOTE: 9 ft. main level walls

An angled snack bar ideally serves the family room and breakfast area.

Built-in window seats add charm to the second-floor bedrooms.

Built-in shelves add functionality to this home's den.

© CARMICHAEL & DAME DESIGNS, INC.

And even though I enjoy my job, there's no sense of freedom or rebellion that seems to surround the aura of an auto mechanic.

flame in ou fireplace? Would ther be a bread machine? Would ther have been newly buil house in 1992 for a young mar ried couple with two childre and another on the way. Would there be a time, like th present, when we realized tha our house is too small?

What I longed for as a adolescent and what I wan today are so far removed from each other, the thoughts seer lifetimes away. Nowadays you'll find my desire for a ne home at the top of my priorit list. The most I get out of th Packers these days is a scarc but precious Monday nigl game or the score I happen t catch on the evening news. I my spare time you'll mor likely find me flipping throug the pages of a home plan boc than Motor Trend.

As my fascinations still tend to go overboard, the search for our "perfect" home has turned into a quest. I know we need a two-story home for the sep aration that is offered between the bedrooms and living areas. A two-story would also allow privacy for

cont'd on next page

♦ SEASONS OF LIFE ~ The SUMMER YEARS ♦

Troon Manor

#28B-9166 Price Code C23

Main Floor: 1649 Sq. Ft.
Second Floor: 712 Sq. Ft.
Total Square Feet: 2361 Sq. Ft.

NOTE: 9 ft. main level walls

A second-floor balcony has a striking view of the bayed living room.

A massive sun deck offers additional living and entertaining space.

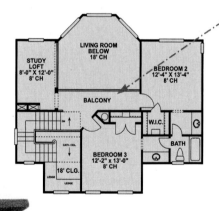

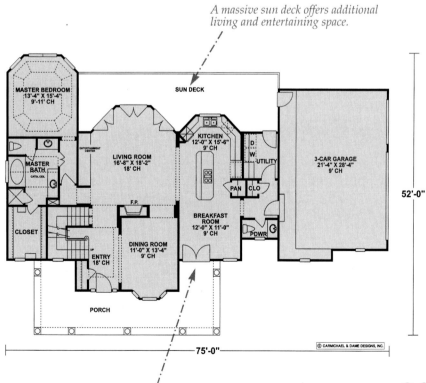

French doors connect the breakfast area to the wrap-around front porch.

I know we need a two-story home for the separation that is offered between the bedrooms and living areas. A two-story would also allow privacy for our children to take naps and to do homework.

our children to take naps and to do homework. It mus[t] also have two separate living spaces so tha[t] our children can have [a] place to g[o] when their friends visit. Plus our home should have a privat[e] sitting room, ideally off th[e] master suite, where my wif[e] and I can read. Along with a[ll] of this, it must also be afford[-]able and a good investment.

This fascination with ne[w] homes isn't really so far o[ff] from my obsession with Bar[t] Starr and the '74 AMX. Although less glamorous, th[e] quest for a new home sti[ll] brings meaning and satisfac[-]tion to my life. Would it b[e] such a far stretch to see ou[r] "dream home" in the contex[t] of high performance? I[ts] make-up? 2,345 total squar[e] feet of horse power comprise[d] of 20,000 board feet of lumbe[r.] Its stats? A four-bedroom[,] two-story brick Colonial wi[th] a basement foundation an[d] three-car garage – ful[ly] equipped, of course. ◆

Calabretta

#28B-4106 Price Code B26

> Main Floor: 1333 Sq. Ft.
> Second Floor: 1280 Sq. Ft.
> Total Square Feet: 2613 Sq. Ft.

NOTE: 9 ft. main level walls

His and her walk-in closets and an extravagant whirlpool tub sets the tone in the master suite.

WHIRLPOOL TUB

CATHEDRAL CEILING

Mbr.
15⁰ x 15⁰
9'-0" CEILING

Br.2
12⁰ x 12⁰

DN

Br.3
13⁰ x 11⁰

L

Br.4
13⁰ x 11⁰

CATHEDRAL CEILING

Unfinished Bonus
21⁸ x 14⁰

Unfinished Bonus Room Adds 323 Sq. Ft.

A huge bonus room has the potential to meet the preferences of many buyers.

Bfst.
11⁰ x 11⁰
SNACK BAR

Fam. Rm.
18⁰ x 15⁰

DESK

Kit.
11⁸ x 12⁰
P.
R.
W. D.

WET BAR
SEAT
DN
UP

OPTIONAL COMPUTER AREA

Liv.
14⁰ x 11⁰

E.

Din.
14⁰ x 11⁰

Gar.
21⁸ x 29⁴

44'-4"

58'-0"

STOOP

© design basics inc.

A wet bar with window seat between the family and living rooms, is also adaptable as a home computer area.

❖ *SEASONS OF LIFE ~The SUMMER YEARS* ❖

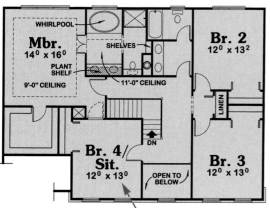

Mbr.
14^0 x 16^0

WHIRLPOOL

SHELVES

PLANT SHELF

9'-0" CEILING

Br. 2
12^0 x 13^2

11'-0" CEILING

LINEN

DN

Br. 4/ Sit.
12^0 x 13^0

OPEN TO BELOW

Br. 3
12^0 x 13^0

Bedroom 4 can be an optional sitting area with access from the master suite.

The large laundry room includes a soaking sink, closet and access to the outside.

Sutter

#28B-4147 Price Code B26

Main Floor:	1357 Sq. Ft.
Second Floor:	1285 Sq. Ft.
Total Square Feet:	2642 Sq. Ft.

NOTE: 9 ft. main level walls

Extra counter space makes it easy to serve meals in the dining room.

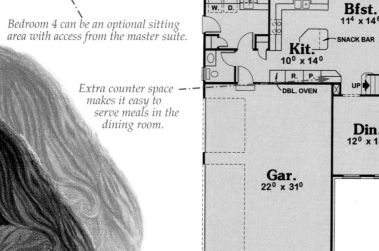
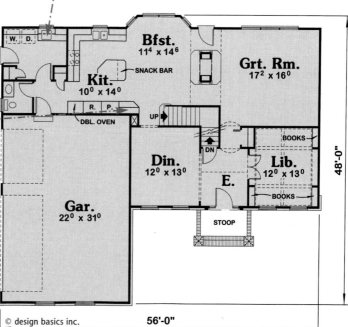

W. D.

Bfst.
11^4 x 14^6

SNACK BAR

Grt. Rm.
17^2 x 16^0

Kit.
10^0 x 14^0

R. P.

DBL. OVEN

UP

BOOKS

DN

Din.
12^0 x 13^0

E.

Lib.
12^0 x 13^0

BOOKS

Gar.
22^0 x 31^0

STOOP

48'-0"

© design basics inc.

56'-0"

It's rare when everyone in our family doesn't have something going on – music practice, a volleyball game or company function. With how busy we are these days, when we are all home at the same time, we end up crowding into the kitchen or family room, whether it be to watch a movie, do homework or cook supper. And when I say "crowding" that's exactly what I mean! What our family needs is openness, especially between the kitchen and family area ...

SOLUTION

The family areas in both of these homes are secluded at the back of the home. Designed for the busy family, the Robins Lane (❶, at right) offers a long, open area that extends from its kitchen to a sunken family room. In the Edgewood, (❷, at left and interior view) the kitchen and family area connect like one large room with a snack bar island serving the dinette and family room.

A screened-in veranda is the perfect extension of the living and dining rooms.

The master bedroom features a bayed sitting area, designed to allow busy parents to unwind.

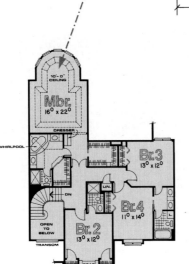

This bayed den makes the perfect home office with its private location and double-door seclusion.

Edgewood

#28B-2839 Price Code B30

Main Floor: 1631 Sq. Ft.
Second Floor: 1426 Sq. Ft.
Total Square Feet: 3057 Sq. Ft.

♦ *SEASONS OF LIFE ~The SUMMER YEARS* ♦

Robins Lane

#28B-8031 Price Code A20

Br. 4
10⁰ x 11⁶

Br. 3
11⁰ x 11⁰

Mbr.
15⁴ x 12⁰

Br. 2
10⁰ x 11⁵

DN

BONUS ROOM
9⁴ x 16⁴

A compartmental bath with soaking tub and shower, completes the master suite.

Bonus Room Adds 165 Sq. Ft.

A large bonus room on the second floor provides a great place for storage off the master suite.

Main Floor: 1046 Sq. Ft.
Second Floor: 983 Sq. Ft.
Total Square Feet: 2029 Sq. Ft.

The open dining and living rooms are designed to be flexible to accommodate guests during the holidays.

Din.
10⁰ x 11⁵

Kit.
9⁸ x 11⁵

SNACK BAR

Bfst.
10⁴ x 12⁰

DN

Fam. rm.
17⁰ x 15⁰

❶

8'-8" CEILING

P.

R.

Liv. rm.
12⁰ x 14⁶

9'-0" CEILING

DN

E.

UP

W. D.

Gar.
21⁴ x 22⁰

COVERED PORCH

40' - 0"

48' - 0"

© design basics inc.

Grt. rm.
18¹ x 14⁰

Bfst.
10⁰ x 12⁵

Kit.
8¹⁰ x 11³

DESK

Din.
10⁰ x 12⁴

Gar.
21³ x 21⁸

COVERED PORCH

40'-0"

44'-0"

© design basics inc.

Br. 2
10⁰ x 11⁶

W/P

Mbr.
12⁰ x 16⁰

LIN.

9'-0" CLG.

DN

10'-0" CLG.

OPEN TO BELOW

Br. 3
10⁰ x 11⁰

PLANTS

A wrapping covered porch is a great place to get away from it all.

This large great room will be perfect for the family, easily connecting with the kitchen and breakfast area.

Main Floor: 891 Sq. F
Second Floor: 759 Sq. F
Total Square Feet: 1650 Sq. F

Laverton

#28B-2248

Price Code B16

...balcony at the top of
...e U-shaped stairway
...ings added spaciousness
...the entry.

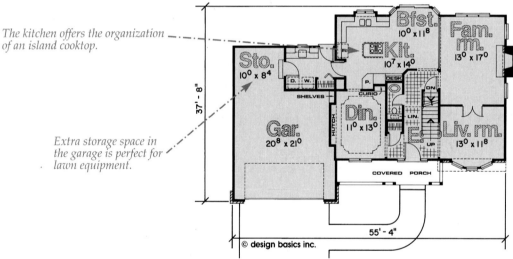

*The kitchen offers the organization
of an island cooktop.*

*Extra storage space in
the garage is perfect for
lawn equipment.*

© design basics inc.

37' - 8"

55' - 4"

Sto. 10⁰ x 8⁴

Gar. 20⁸ x 21⁰

Bfst. 10⁰ x 11⁸

Kit. 10⁷ x 14⁰

Fam. rm. 13⁰ x 17⁰

Din. 11⁰ x 13⁰

Liv. rm. 13⁰ x 11⁸

COVERED PORCH

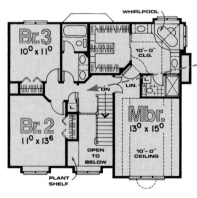

WHIRLPOOL

Br. 3 10⁰ x 11⁰

10'-0" CLG.

Br. 2 11⁰ x 13⁶

Mbr. 13⁰ x 15⁰

10'-0" CEILING

OPEN TO BELOW

PLANT SHELF

*A second-floor balcony overlooks
the entry with plant shelf.*

Oakbrook

#28B-2619

Price Code B19

Main Floor:	1093 Sq. Ft.
Second Floor:	905 Sq. Ft.
Total Square Feet:	1998 Sq. Ft.

SITUATION

Our children are the most important things in our lives. Making their childhood an enjoyable experience is our number one focus. Because of the many activities they're involved in, their rooms could use built-in shelves to display their trophies and event photographs. Their school work is also very important. And because of the noise that just naturally exists with a family, we need their bedrooms to be separate from the living areas so they have a quiet place to study. . .

Bedroom 3 has unique features, such as twin closets, an arched window and a 10-foot-high ceiling.

SOLUTION

Bedroom 4 in the Crawford (❶, at left and interior view), offers a built-in desk to provide children with secluded place to do homework. A large bookshelf, (❷, at right) in Bedroom 4 of the Hartford provides a place to show off medallions, trophies, memorabilia and photographs.

The openness between the kitchen, hearth room and breakfast area allows the family to interact while preparing dinner.

A built-in entertainment center in the great room is convenient for home electronic equipment.

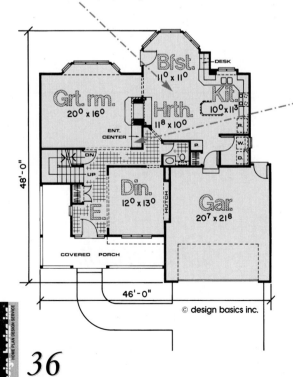

© design basics inc.

Crawford

#28B-2408 Price Code B22

Main Floor: 1150 Sq. Ft.
Second Floor: 1120 Sq. Ft.
Total Square Feet: 2270 Sq. Ft.

♦ SEASONS OF LIFE ~The SUMMER YEARS ♦

All three second-floor bedrooms offer walk-in closets.

Hartford

#28B-2458 Price Code B29

A built-in entertainment center in the hearth room makes it an informal place to relax.

| Main Floor: 2084 Sq. Ft. |
| Second Floor: 848 Sq. Ft. |
| Total Square Feet: 2932 Sq. Ft. |

Br. 4 12⁰ x 13⁰

Br. 2 12⁰ x 14⁰ 10' - 0" CEILING

Br. 3 12⁰ x 14⁰

BOOKS

LIN.

DN

COVERED VERANDA

WHIRLPOOL

SKYLIGHTS

Grt. rm. 18⁰ x 18⁰ 11'- 8" CEILING

Hrth. 12⁷ x 15³ ENT CENTER

Bfst. 11³ x 11³ SNACK BAR

Mbr. 16³ x 14⁰ 10' - 0" CEILING

Kit. 12⁹ x 12⁸

UP DN

Den 13³ x 14⁰ 10'- 4" CLG.

Din. 12⁰ x 15⁰

Gar. 21³ x 31³

COVERED STOOP

TRANSOMS

© design basics inc.

68' - 8"

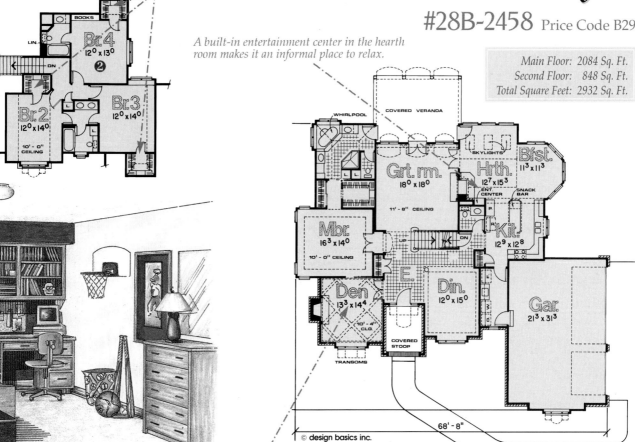

The den, distinguished with a fireplace, becomes a private retreat off the master suite through a pocket door.

ORDER DIRECT· (800) 947-7526

SITUATION

Our home and life-style consist of activity. I wouldn't have it any other way, except for the fact that within our current home, I have no place for a few moments of privacy. Either someone's watching a television show in the family room or doing homework in the kitchen or working in the den. Even if it were just before bedtime, it sure would be great to have a place where I could spend some time by myself...

SOLUTION

The elegant Wilks Manor features a covered porch accessible from the master suite (❶, at far right). Located away from other areas of the home, it is the perfect place to unwind. An angled sitting room adjoins the master suite in the Magrath (❷, at right). At the end of the day, it is a great spot to read before bedtime or quietly chat with a spouse.

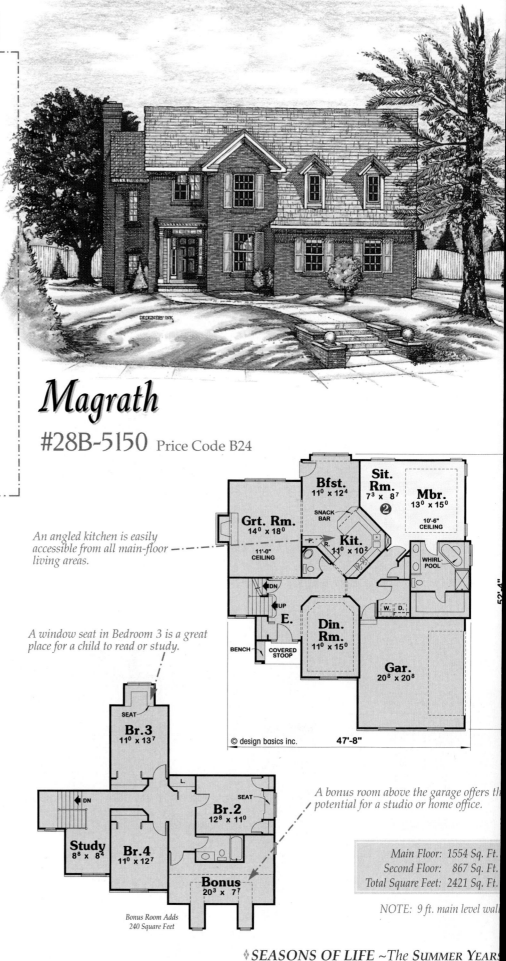

Magrath

#28B-5150 Price Code B24

An angled kitchen is easily accessible from all main-floor living areas.

A window seat in Bedroom 3 is a great place for a child to read or study.

A bonus room above the garage offers the potential for a studio or home office.

Bfst. 11⁰ x 12⁴

Sit. Rm. 7³ x 8⁷ ❷

Mbr. 13⁰ x 15⁰ 10'-6" CEILING

Grt. Rm. 14⁰ x 18⁰ 11'-0" CEILING

SNACK BAR

Kit. 11⁰ x 10²

WHIRL POOL

W. D.

DN

UP

E.

Din. Rm. 11⁰ x 15⁰

BENCH

COVERED STOOP

Gar. 20⁸ x 20⁸

© design basics inc.   47'-8"   52'-4"

SEAT

Br.3 11⁰ x 13⁷

SEAT

Br.2 12⁸ x 11⁰

DN

Study 8⁸ x 8⁴

Br.4 11⁰ x 12⁷

Bonus 20³ x 7⁷

Bonus Room Adds 240 Square Feet

Main Floor: 1554 Sq. Ft.
Second Floor: 867 Sq. Ft.
Total Square Feet: 2421 Sq. Ft.

NOTE: 9 ft. main level wall

A cathedral ceiling towers over the family room, which is open to the kitchen and breakfast room.

A private guest suite on the main floor is a great "flex" room, offering the possibility to use it as a home office or in-law suite.

Future expansion space above the garage offers additional storage to the home.

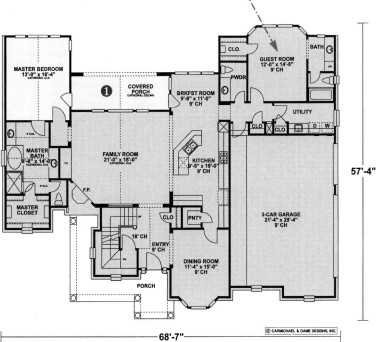

Wilks Manor

#28B-9165 Price Code C26

Main Floor: 2087 Sq. Ft.
Second Floor: 552 Sq. Ft.
Total Square Feet: 2639 Sq. Ft.

NOTE: 9 ft. main level walls

KID AREAS . . .
Key areas in today's homes are those reserved for childrens' activities. Whether used as a playroom for small children or a computer loft for homework and games, these flexible areas provide a retreat for children and ample room for their activities. The highlighted areas in the following plans cater to children's needs and interests.

PARENT-SUPERVISED HOMEWORK

Main Floor: 845 Sq. Ft.	
Second Floor: 760 Sq. Ft.	
Total Square Feet 1605 Sq. Ft.	

Arbor
#28B-2526 Price Code B16

A striking, sloped ceiling and warm fireplace make a dramatic presentation in the living areas.

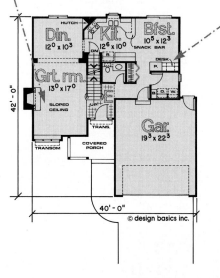

Convenient for children to do homework with parents nearby, a planning desk is located in the breakfast area.

Double doors access the volume master suite, with a second set of French doors leading to a private dressing area.

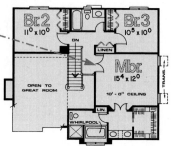

USEABLE FLEX SPACE

Main Floor: 1240 Sq. Ft.	
Second Floor: 1283 Sq. Ft.	
Total Square Feet: 2523 Sq. Ft.	

Emery
#28B-4125 Price Code B25

NOTE: 9 ft. main level walls

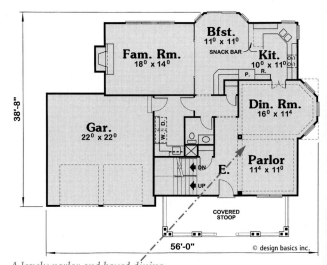

A lovely parlor and bayed dining room create a welcoming view from the entry.

The master suite is uniquely planned, with a dresser alcove and sunny window seat located between the master bath and large walk-in closet.

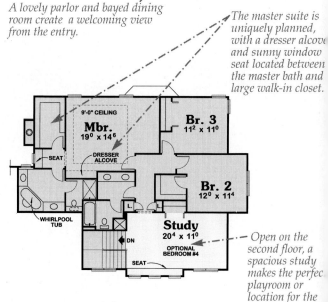

Open on the second floor, a spacious study makes the perfect playroom or location for the family computer.

SEASONS OF LIFE ~The SUMMER YEARS

CHOICE COMPUTER AREA

Main Floor:	1002 Sq. Ft.
Second Floor:	926 Sq. Ft.
Total Square Feet:	1928 Sq. Ft.

Branford
#28B-5085 Price Code B19

NOTE: 9 ft. main level walls

Separating the warm hearth room and living room is a see-thru fireplace and back-to-back bookshelves.

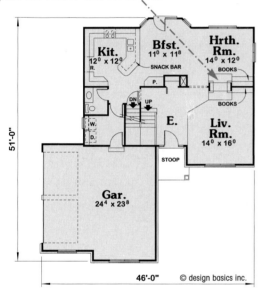

A cozy computer area at the top of the stairs provides a quiet area for schoolwork or surfing the internet.

A large unfinished bonus room would be ideal as a playroom or for convenient storage.

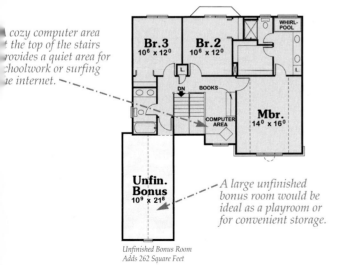

Unfinished Bonus Room Adds 262 Square Feet

WELL-APPOINTED GAMEROOM

Main Floor:	1162 Sq. Ft.
Second Floor:	1255 Sq. Ft.
Total Square Feet:	2417 Sq. Ft.

Patagonia
#28B-5086 Price Code B24

NOTE: 9 ft. main level walls

A rear covered porch is a great place to spend a few quiet moments alone.

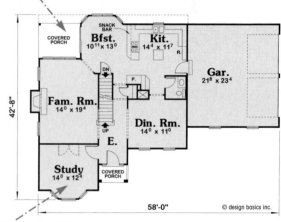

A bayed study is located just off the entry and has optional double doors connecting the spacious family room.

Among other options, unfinished storage space on the second floor is easily converted into a gameroom for children of any age.

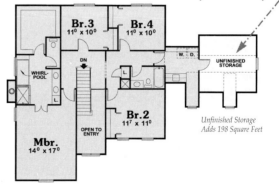

Unfinished Storage Adds 198 Square Feet

FUN CHILD'S PLAYROOM

Main Floor:	1322 Sq. Ft.
Second Floor:	1272 Sq. Ft.
Total Square Feet:	2594 Sq. Ft.

Newberry

#28B-1455 Price Code B25

WELL-PLACED TOY CLOSET

Main Floor:	866 Sq. Ft.
Second Floor:	905 Sq. Ft.
Total Square Feet:	1771 Sq. Ft.

Paige

#28B-3581 Price Code B17

Bicycles, large toys or lawn equipment are easily kept in a large storage space in the garage.

A bright sun room just off the breakfast area makes a cheery retreat and has access to the outside.

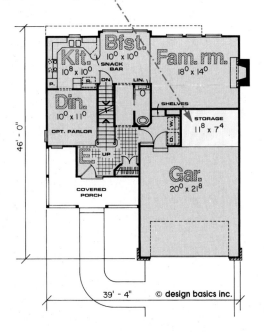

© design basics inc.

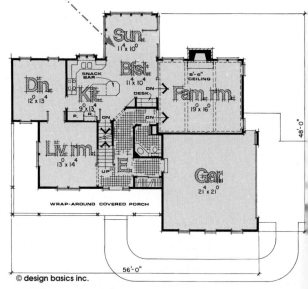

© design basics inc.

A window seat in bedroom 2 is a relaxing place for a child.

A second-floor laundry room with a soaking sink is conveniently near the bedrooms.

Located off one of the secondary bedrooms, an optional play area perfect for toy storage as well as desk for homework.

Finishing off an optional toy closet in lieu of a two-story entry could provide needed storage space for a growing family.

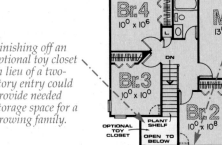

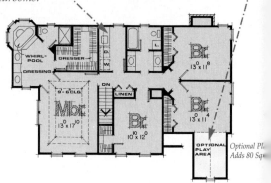

❖ *SEASONS OF LIFE ~The SUMMER YEARS*

HOMEWORK HAVENS

Main Floor:	976 Sq. Ft.
Second Floor:	823 Sq. Ft.
Total Square Feet:	1799 Sq. Ft.

Francis
#28B-2952   Price Code B17

A cozy covered deck is located off the breakfast area and has a view from the parlor through transom windows.

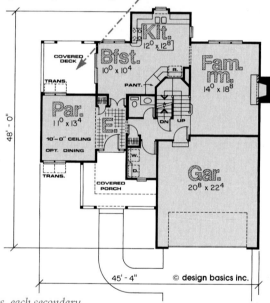

...irs, each secondary ...om has a handy ...in desk.

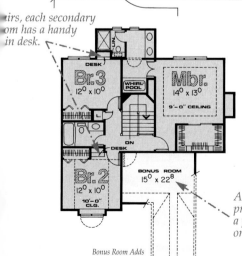

A large bonus room provides options for a playroom, storage or another bedroom.

Bonus Room Adds 274 Square Feet

SPACE FOR STUDYING

Main Floor:	1214 Sq. Ft.
Second Floor:	1118 Sq. Ft.
Total Square Feet:	2332 Sq. Ft.

NOTE: 9 ft. main level walls

Ainsley
#28B-4145   Price Code B23

A walk-in pantry offers additional storage to the kitchen.

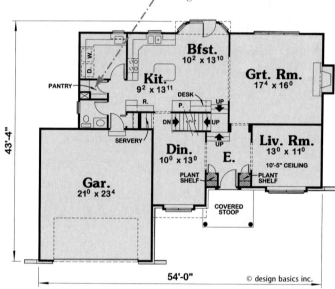

Bedroom 2 features a built-in desk, great for schoolwork or computer games.

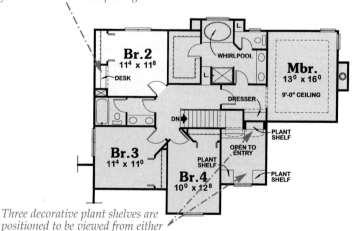

Three decorative plant shelves are positioned to be viewed from either the entry or the second level.

FLEX SPACE . . . An appealing element in determining the value of a home is the adaptability of its rooms. How easily they can change to meet the needs of today's family is key in determining the efficiency and functionality of the home. Below are a number of designs that meet the expectations of a buyer in search of valuable "flex space."

QUAINT HOME OFFICE

| Main Floor: 1475 Sq. Ft. |
| Second Floor: 1085 Sq. Ft. |
| Total Square Feet: 2560 Sq. Ft. |

Suffolk
#28B-5037 Price Code B25

NOTE: 9 ft. main level walls

Easily the most unique room in this home, bedroom 4 could be converted to a private home office with twin bookshelves surrounding a window seat.

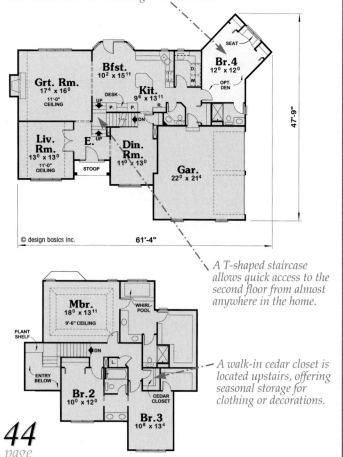

A T-shaped staircase allows quick access to the second floor from almost anywhere in the home.

A walk-in cedar closet is located upstairs, offering seasonal storage for clothing or decorations.

SUNNY DEN VIEW

| Main Floor: 1005 Sq. Ft. |
| Second Floor: 1052 Sq. Ft. |
| Total Square Feet: 2057 Sq. Ft. |

Boulder Point
#28B-8112 Price Code A20

Offering the option of being converted to a cozy den, the dining room enjoys a view onto the covered front porch.

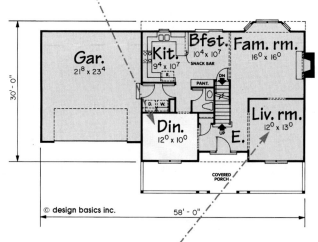

The living room opens to the large family room, creating a natural expansion space when entertaining.

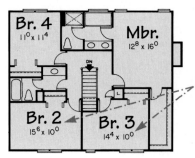

Upstairs, bedrooms 2 and 3 are large enough to accommodate children's playthings.

VERSATILE FORMAL ROOM

Main Floor: 840 Sq. Ft.
Second Floor: 768 Sq. Ft.
Total Square Feet: 1608 Sq. Ft.

Apple Woods
#28B-8109 Price Code A16

Main Floor: 866 Sq. Ft.
Second Floor: 788 Sq. Ft.
Total Square Feet: 1654 Sq. Ft.

Harbor Lane
#28B-8139 Price Code A16

A rear staircase makes the second floor easily accessible.

A grand family area including the kitchen and family room has key elements such as a snack bar and fireplace to ensure comfortable day-to-day living.

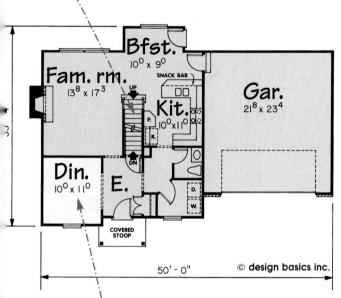

Bfst. 10⁰ x 9⁰
Fam. rm. 13⁸ x 17³
Gar. 21⁸ x 23⁴
Kit. 10⁰ x 11⁰
Din. 10⁰ x 11⁰
COVERED STOOP
50' - 0"
© design basics inc.

The versatile dining room, as viewed from the entry, has the option of becoming a very secluded home office or den.

By closing it off from the kitchen and adding double doors from the entry, the dining room could be a private home office.

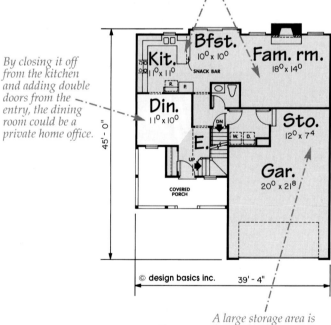

Kit. 9⁰ x 11⁰
Bfst. 10⁰ x 10⁰
Fam. rm. 18⁰ x 14⁰
Din. 11⁰ x 10⁰
Sto. 12⁰ x 7⁴
Gar. 20⁰ x 21⁸
COVERED PORCH
45' - 0"
© design basics inc.   39' - 4"

A large storage area is featured in the garage, perfect for lawn and sporting equipment.

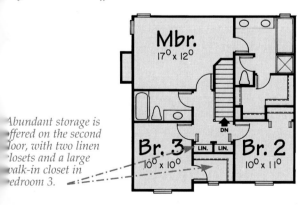

Mbr. 17⁰ x 12⁰
Br. 3 10⁰ x 10⁰
Br. 2 10⁰ x 11⁰

Abundant storage is offered on the second floor, with two linen closets and a large walk-in closet in bedroom 3.

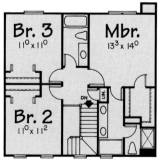

Br. 3 11⁰ x 11⁰
Mbr. 13³ x 14⁰
Br. 2 11⁰ x 11²

DINING ROOM DUALITY

Main Floor: 904 Sq. Ft.
Second Floor: 796 Sq. Ft.
Total Square Feet: 1700 Sq. Ft.

Ashworth

#28B-3103 Price Code B17

BENEFICIAL BEDROOM/OFFICE

Main Floor: 845 Sq. Ft.
Second Floor: 883 Sq. Ft.
Total Square Feet: 1728 Sq. Ft.

Deming

#28B-2545 Price Code B17

Near the kitchen and great room, the dining room features a uniquely-shaped hutch space, and could be an exquisite sunroom with additional windows.

Located off the great room and kitchen, the dining room could easily be converted to an office area.

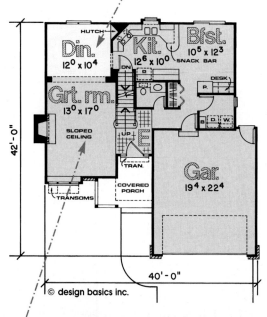

The great room has a sloped ceiling and lovely transom windows viewing the front yard.

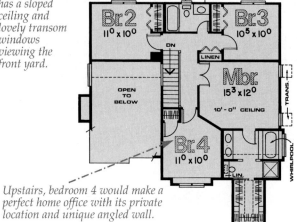

Upstairs, bedroom 4 would make a perfect home office with its private location and unique angled wall.

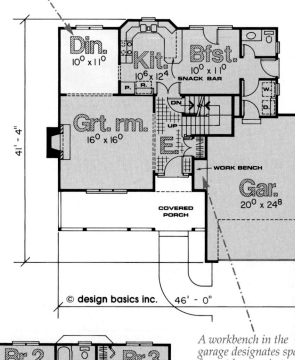

A workbench in the garage designates spa[ce] for outdoor projects.

His and her walk-in closets add to this pampering master suite.

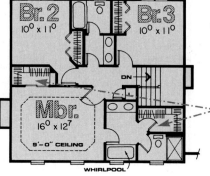

❖SEASONS OF LIFE ~The SUMMER YEARS

FRONT ROOM FLEXIBILITY

Main Floor: 927 Sq. Ft.	
Second Floor: 865 Sq. Ft.	
Total Square Feet: 1792 Sq. Ft.	

Hackett

#28B-3383 Price Code B17

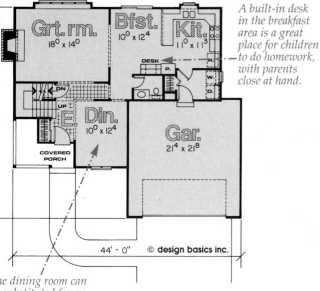

A built-in desk in the breakfast area is a great place for children to do homework, with parents close at hand.

he dining room can substituted for an egant parlor and is penly viewed from e entry.

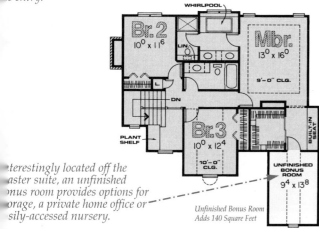

terestingly located off the aster suite, an unfinished nus room provides options for orage, a private home office or sily-accessed nursery.

Unfinished Bonus Room Adds 140 Square Feet

FAMILY COMPUTER LOCATION

Main Floor: 1098 Sq. Ft.	
Second Floor: 1184 Sq. Ft.	
Total Square Feet: 2282 Sq. Ft.	

Eldon

#28B-4105 Price Code B22

NOTE: 9 ft. main level walls

A large family area is located on the main level, with close ties to the kitchen and breakfast area.

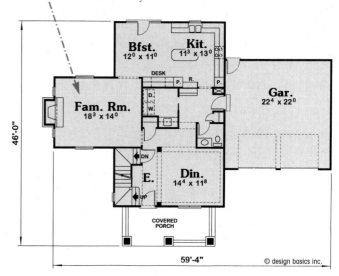

Window seats are featured in bedrooms 2 and 3, which are served by a full bath.

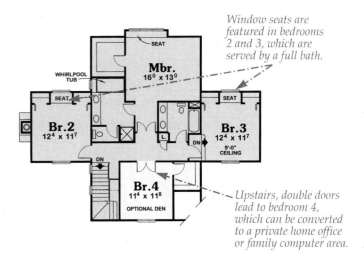

Upstairs, double doors lead to bedroom 4, which can be converted to a private home office or family computer area.

The Home My Mother Inspired

Her prize was an elegant dining room table and china cabinet that was given to her by my father. And if there was a lack of furniture throughout the rest of the home, I would have never known...

Of all the things that have inspired me about my mother, none have affected me quite so deeply, as the home she created for us kids.

To this day, I'm not quite sure how she did it. Our Carlsbad, New Mexico home was nothing extravagant, mind you. It was, in fact, a small three bedroom, one-story home that barely accommodated my mother, five brothers and sisters and me. But Mom somehow made it feel special. Perhaps it was a combination of her strict code of cleanliness or her unique decorating style that made us feel comfortable and welcome in each room. It could have even been her seasonal ritual of moving the furniture around, making our small home seem new again and again. Or that, in spite of the fact we would "crowd" the home by today's standards, she made it feel spacious.

Even though we didn't have a lot of money to spend on fancy furnishings, she made each piece within our home seem as though it was specifically designed for its spot. Her prize was an elegant dining room table and china cabinet that was given to her by my father. And if there was a lack of furniture throughout the rest of the home, I would have never known it, since my mother's love of greenery resulted in plants tastefully displayed in any otherwise sparse area of the home.

While everyone has bragging rights when it comes to their mother, our sense of the magical comfort she created wasn't perceived solely by us. Growing up, all of our friends and neighbors also wanted to be at our home. From grade school to high school, the home of choice for studying, slumber parties or after-school hanging out, was ours. All of my friends soon called her "Mom," thinking her the "hippest" parent in town because she listened to Motley Crue along with us.

Though many of my fondest memories with-

cont'd on next page

Saybrooke

#28B-5003 Price Code B27

Total Square Feet: 2750 Sq. Ft.

NOTE: 9 ft. main level walls

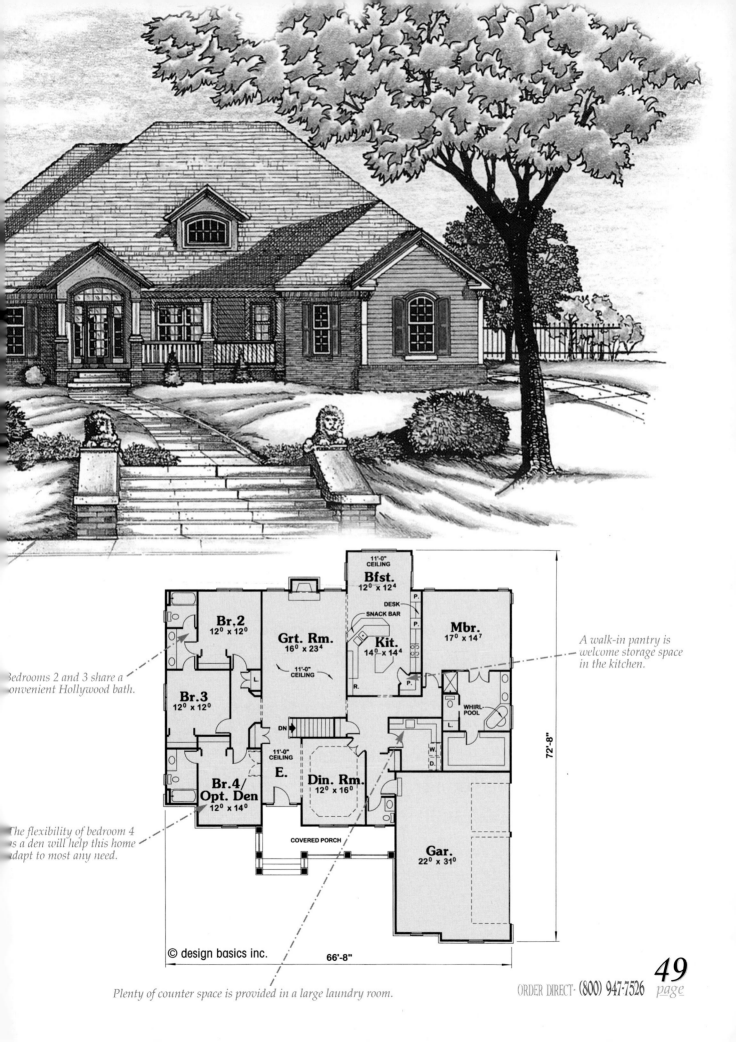

Bedrooms 2 and 3 share a convenient Hollywood bath.

A walk-in pantry is welcome storage space in the kitchen.

The flexibility of bedroom 4 as a den will help this home adapt to most any need.

Br.2 12⁰ x 12⁰

Br.3 12⁰ x 12⁰

Br.4/ Opt. Den 12⁰ x 14⁰

Grt. Rm. 16⁰ x 23⁴

11'-0" CEILING

E.

11'-0" CEILING

Din. Rm. 12⁰ x 16⁰

COVERED PORCH

Bfst. 12⁰ x 12⁴

11'-0" CEILING

DESK

SNACK BAR

Kit. 14⁰ x 14⁴

Mbr. 17⁰ x 14⁷

WHIRL-POOL

W.
D.

Gar. 22⁰ x 31⁰

72'-8"

66'-8"

© design basics inc.

Plenty of counter space is provided in a large laundry room.

Holden

#28B-4998 Price Code B22

Total Square Feet: 2227 Sq. Ft.

NOTE: 9 ft. main level walls

The openness between the kitchen, breakfast area and great room is designed for family interaction.

Extra storage space for bikes and lawn equipment is provided in the garage.

Mbr.
13⁰ x 15⁶

Grt. Rm.
16⁰ x 20⁰

Bfst.
10⁰ x 13⁸

Kit.
11⁰ x 13⁸

Gar.
21⁰ x 21⁴

DESK

P. R.

WHIRL-POOL

L.

DN

Stor.

W. D.

Br. 2
11⁰ x 12⁰

Br. 3/
Opt.
Liv. Rm.
12⁰ x 11⁰

E.

Din.
Rm.
12⁰ x 15⁵

Office/
Opt.
Br. 4
11⁰ x 13⁵

COVERED PORCH

48'-8"

76'-8"

© design basics inc.

An office with access to the outside is perfect for a home-based business.

Growing up, all of our friends and neighbors also wanted to be at our home. From grade school to high school, the home of choice for studying and slumber parties was ours.

in our home are of my mother, the sense of security and welcome she imparted still existed the many times she was not there. A divorced parent, spending long hours working towards her nursing degree, she oftentimes was not home with us. Yet our home nurtured us in her place. It provided comfort and strength when she wasn't there and helped us understand that her rules still applied in her absence.

Somehow, and with little fanfare, she gave us a home that both cultivated our fledgling souls and inspired us to greatness.

Having long since moved away from my old New Mexico home, my family and I are ready to move from our current residence into a larger home to accommodate our two children and a new baby on the way. As I draw up a detailed list of "must have's" in preparation to build our next home, it's apparent to me now, more than ever, that what I really want, is a home like the one my mother created for me.

cont'd on next page

❖ *SEASONS OF LIFE ~The SUMMER YEARS* ❖

Fayette

#28B-2346 Price Code B24

Main Floor: 1369 Sq. Ft.
Second Floor: 1111 Sq. Ft.
Total Square Feet: 2480 Sq. Ft.

The sunken family room in this home is easily accessed from both the kitchen and entry.

The living and dining room easily expand into each other when entertaining.

Built-in shelves offer a place to display momentos in the den.

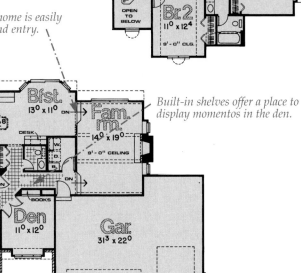

© design basics inc.

Ascott

#28B-3057 Price Code B25

Total Square Feet: 2538 Sq. Ft.

Built-in dressers free space in the master bedroom for a couple of chairs by a bayed window.

A covered porch off the laundry room is a great place to relax when taking a break from housework.

WHIRLPOOL

TRAPS

GLASS BLOCK

BUILT - IN DRESSERS

TRANSOMS

Bfst.
9'-0" CLG.

Fam. rm.
19⁰ x 17⁴

CATHEDRAL CEILING

Mbr.
13⁰ x 20⁴
9'-0" CEILING

Din.
16⁰ x 13⁰
12'-0" CEILING

SNACK BAR

Kit.
14⁴ x 14⁸

COVERED PORCH

SHELVES

64' - 8"

Br. 2
13⁰ x 11⁰

Liv. rm.
13⁴ x 16⁰
10'-0" CEILING

Br. 3
11⁰ x 13⁰

OPTIONAL DEN
10'-0" CEILING

Gar.
22⁴ x 31⁴

TRANSOMS

COVERED PORCH

TRANSOMS

© design basics inc.

68' - 8"

Bedroom 2 is flexible as a den just off the entry.

More than I want a large family room or tons of closet and storage space, I want my children to fondly remember their days spent playing make-believe in the kitchen and board games in the bedrooms.

I realize that more than I want my children to have their own bedrooms, I want them to love coming home to a clean, welcoming house after school, as I did. I want them to be as proud to bring their friends into their home as I was. More than I want a large family room or tons of closet and storage space, I want my children to fondly remember their days spent playing make believe in the kitchen and board games in the bedrooms. More than I want a luxurious master suite with a soaking tub, I want a haven, a place I can shape and give its own unique character, as my mother did. More than I want office space, I desire to give my family her comforting sense of home. More than I desire a large, open kitchen with lots of counter space, I desire a place where my husband, children and I will enjoy being together. More than I desire a dining room in which to serve holiday dinners, I want my children

cont'd on next page

◆ *SEASONS OF LIFE ~The SUMMER YEARS* ◆

Arant

#28B-2261 Price Code B24

Separated from main-floor activity, three comfortably-sized secondary bedrooms share a full compartmented bath with dual-sink vanity.

| Main Floor: 1733 Sq. Ft. |
| Second Floor: 672 Sq. Ft. |
| Total Square Feet: 2405 Sq. Ft. |

The impressive great room offers tall windows that flood its spaciousness with natural light.

The large kitchen welcomes the whole family with plenty of working counter space and open access to a warm hearth room.

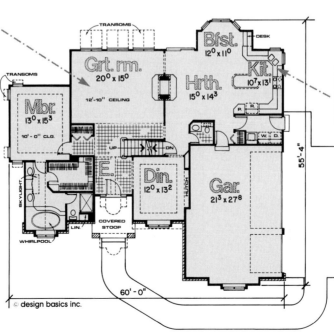

Br.3 12⁰ x 11⁶
Br.2 13⁷ x 11⁰
Br.4 11⁰ x 12²
OPEN TO BELOW

Grt. rm. 20⁰ x 15⁰
12'-10" CEILING
Bfst. 12⁰ x 11⁰
Hrth. 15⁰ x 14³
Kit. 10⁷ x 13¹
Mbr. 13⁰ x 15³
10'-0" CLG.
Din. 12⁰ x 13²
Gar. 21³ x 27⁸
55'-4"
60'-0"
COVERED STOOP
WHIRLPOOL
SKYLIGHT
TRANSOMS

© design basics inc.

to experience the warm togetherness and sharing that my mother's traditional Sunday Spanish brunches – refried beans, eggs, bacon, sausage, chili con queso, tortillas, coffee and iced tea – brought to my family.

More than I want the separate bedrooms to give my kids their individuality, I want them to grow up, as we did, with a deep closeness and bond fostered by their "casa." More than I desire additional space, I desire a place where my family can "catch up" – a place where we all come together at one point in our busy day. I want a place that, if only in my dreams, will remind me of the honeysuckle-smelling mornings and deep starry nights of New Mexico. And even more than I care about all of this, I care about creating a home as my mother did – a home that will make us content. A home that will make us happy to live in it. ◆

Lancaster

#28B-1752 Price Code B18

Main Floor:	919 Sq. Ft.
Second Floor:	927 Sq. Ft.
Total Square Feet:	1846 Sq. Ft.

His and her closets bring convenience to the master suite.

Mbr. 12⁰ x 16⁰ · 9'-4" CEILING
Br. 10⁰ x 11⁶
Br. 10⁰ x 11⁶
WHIRLPOOL
Br. 10⁰ x 11 · 10'-0" CEILING
OPEN TO BELOW
PLANT SHELF
LIN.
DN

Openness is maintained between the kitchen and great room via a half wall.

This home's large wrap-around porch welcomes a porch swing or outdoor furniture.

Kit. 9⁰ x 11
Bfst. 10⁰ x 16⁰
Grt. rm. 18⁰ x 14⁰
Dn. 10⁰ x 13⁰
Gar. 20⁰ x 19⁸
40'-0"
44'-0"
WRAPAROUND PORCH
DN · UP

© design basics inc.

❖ *SEASONS OF LIFE ~The SUMMER YEARS* ❖

Plainview

#28B-2222 Price Code B20

Total Square Feet: 2068 Sq. Ft.

A covered deck becomes a private retreat off the master suite.

A three-sided fireplace warms the great room, hearthroom and breakfast area.

Flexible as a third bedroom, a secluded den is found just inside the entry.

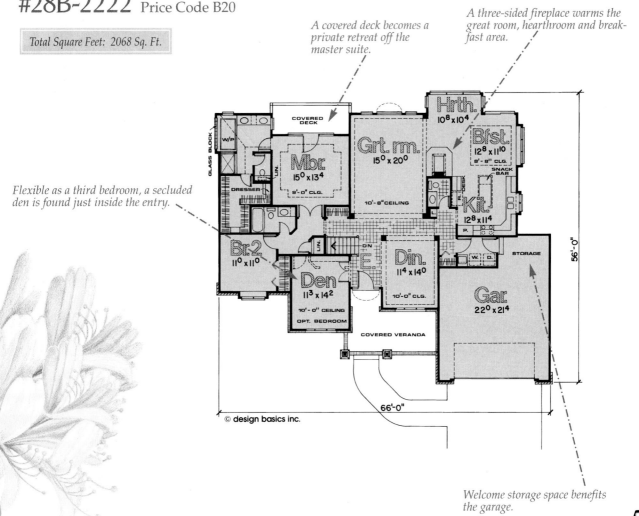

Welcome storage space benefits the garage.

BUILT BY: *BLAKE HOMES*
PHOTO BY: *DESIGN BASICS INC.*

The home in this photograph may be altered from the original plan.

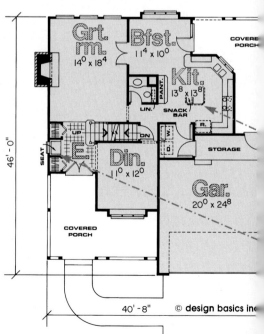

A window seat in bedroom 2 is a great place for a child to read or play.

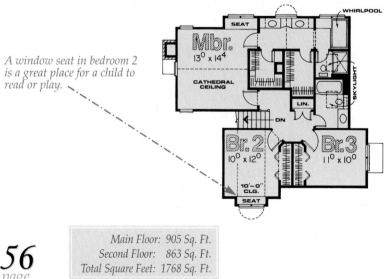

Main Floor: 905 Sq. Ft.
Second Floor: 863 Sq. Ft.
Total Square Feet: 1768 Sq. Ft.

❖ *SEASONS OF LIFE ~The SUMMER YEARS*

Essex

#28B-2213 Price Code B21

A striking family room benefits from its seclusion from the entry and its easy access to the kitchen and breakfast area.

Fam.
16⁰ x 15⁰
9' - 0" CEILING

Bfst.
12⁴ x 11⁰

TRANSOMS

Br. 2
11⁰ x 12⁷

DESK
SNACK BAR

Liv. rm.
14⁰ x 15⁰
10' - 0" CEILING

Kit.
12⁴ x 10⁰

Br. 3
11² x 12⁰
OPTIONAL DEN

LIN.

WHIRL POOL

9' - 0" CEILING

Din.
11⁰ x 13⁰

E.

D. W.

LIN.

DN

Mbr.
16⁰ x 14⁰
10' - 0" CEILING

TRANSOM

10' - 0" CLG.

CVRD. STOOP

Gar.
31³ x 21⁸

54'-0"

70'-0"

© design basics inc.

Separate bedroom wings contribute to privacy for both the master suite and secondary bedrooms.

Bedroom 3 has its own walk-in closet and is flexible as a den.

Torrey

#28B-3096
Price Code B17

A large island kitchen features plenty of counter space for preparing meals.

A window seat brings a sense of nostalgia to the front entry.

Total Square Feet: 2149 Sq. Ft.

Indian Springs

#28B-8059 Price Code A18

Total Square Feet: 1842 Sq. Ft.

To our family, the kitchen is very important. Not only do I need adequate working space to cook, but also need extra room because inevitably, my husband or one of the kids wants to help. And they're not "spoiling the broth," so to speak, they're hanging out there telling me about work or who told Andrea what about so-and-so. I also need a lot of counter space for my small appliances, such as my new bread machine and cappuccino maker, not to mention the toaster. . .

SOLUTION

Both of these accommodating designs offer plenty of counter space for small appliances. The Gerard (❶, at right and interior view), provides an island counter which helps serve as a central point between the stove, refrigerator and sink. The kitchen in the Indian Springs (❷, at left) is also designed with extra spaciousness and features a 10-foot-high ceiling.

A separate laundry room provides a soaking sink and is well-lit by a window.

Mbr.
13⁰ x 15⁰

Grt. rm.
15⁰ x 20⁰
10'-0" CEILING

Bfst.
10⁰ x 12⁰
10'-0" CLG.

Kit.
9⁰ x 13⁰
❷

Br. 2
11⁰ x 11⁴

Br. 3
11⁰ x 11⁰
9'-0" CEILING

E.

Din.
11⁰ x 13⁰
10'-0" CEILING

Gar.
20⁸ x 23⁰

COVERED PORCH

48' - 0"

62' - 0"

© design basics inc.

Both secondary bedrooms are secluded from the main living areas and are near the master suite.

A 10-foot-high ceiling in the dining room brings a sense of spaciousness to this formal room.

✦ **SEASONS OF LIFE** ~The **SUMMER YEARS** ✦

Gerard

#28B-4135 Price Code B23

Main Floor: 1199 Sq. Ft.
Second Floor: 1150 Sq. Ft.
Total Square Feet: 2349 Sq. Ft.

NOTE: 9 ft. main level walls

Bedroom 2 with its own private bath makes the perfect guest bedroom or in-law suite.

Unfinished space above the garage provides welcome additional storage to the second floor.

A wet bar in the family room is convenient when entertaining formally or informally.

Second Floor Plan
Mbr. 15⁰ x 14⁰ — 9'-0" CEILING
Br. 2 11⁰ x 12⁸
DN
Br. 4 10⁰ x 13¹⁰
UNFINISHED STORAGE
Br. 3 11⁰ x 12⁰

Unfinished Storage Adds 274 Square Feet

Main Floor Plan
44'-0"
Fam. Rm. 18⁰ x 14⁰
WET BAR
Bfst. 11⁰ x 10⁰
Kit. 10⁰ x 12⁸
P. R.
DN / UP
Liv. Rm. 11⁰ x 14⁰
E.
Din. Rm. 10⁴ x 13⁶
Gar. 20⁸ x 22⁰
COVERED STOOP
50'-0"
© design basics inc.

BUILT BY: *RLR CONSTRUCTION*
PHOTO BY: *DESIGN BASICS INC.*

The island kitchen features an abundance of natural light through transom windows.

The dining room is served by a convenient wet bar/servery.

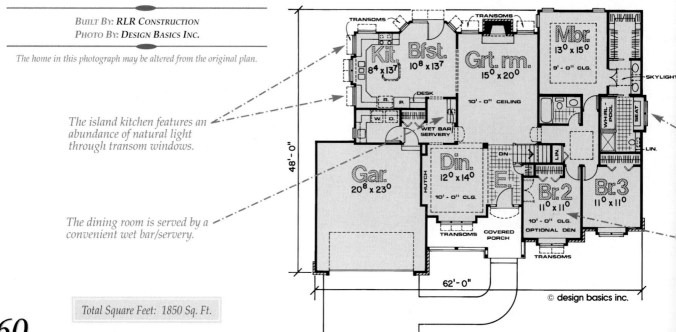

Kit. 8⁴ x 13⁷

Bfst. 10⁸ x 13⁷

Grt. rm. 15⁰ x 20⁰
10' - 0" CEILING

Mbr. 13⁰ x 15⁰
9' - 0" CLG.

DESK

WET BAR SERVERY

W. D.

SKYLIGHT

WH-RL-POOL

SEAT

Gar. 20⁸ x 23⁰

Din. 12⁰ x 14⁰
10' - 0" CLG.

DN

LIN

Br. 2 11⁰ x 11⁰
10' - 0" CLG.
OPTIONAL DEN

Br. 3 11⁰ x 11⁰

HUTCH

TRANSOMS

COVERED PORCH

TRANSOMS

48' - 0"

62' - 0"

© design basics inc.

Total Square Feet: 1850 Sq. Ft.

❖ *SEASONS OF LIFE ~The SUMMER YEAR.*

Shawnee

#28B-2461

Price Code B18

A sunny window seat in the master bath helps assist one when getting ready.

Bedroom 2 is flexible as a den or other living space.

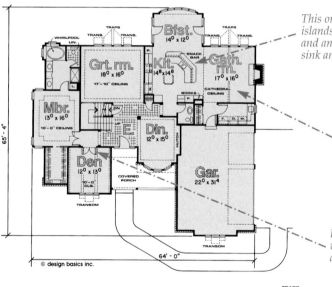

This organized kitchen features two islands, one with a huge snack bar and another to shorten trips to the sink and stove.

A cathedral ceiling and tall windows characterize the gathering room, just off the kitchen.

Double doors reveal the den with volume ceiling – perfect for a home work center.

Main Floor: 2158 Sq. Ft.
Second Floor: 821 Sq. Ft.
Total Square Feet: 2979 Sq. Ft.

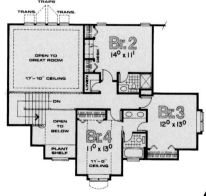

Appleton

#28B-2800 Price Code B29

I made a decision early on as a parent to be home to raise my children. Of course, the consequence of doing so is that it's not only a financial risk, but also a career risk. As a result, I've decided to work out of my home to bring in extra money and also to keep my skills sharp for when I return to the "traditional" workforce. I'm finding it hard, however, to keep any semblance of order with my work spread out on the kitchen table. It sure would be nice to have a home office. . .

Coopers Farm

#28B-8045 Price Code A21

Total Square Feet: 2151 Sq. Ft.

The kitchen boasts plenty of counter space for small appliances and working surface for preparing meals.

TRANSOMS

Mbr. 13⁰ x 16⁵

Grt. rm. 16⁰ x 20⁰

Bfst. 10⁰ x 11⁴

Kit. 8¹⁰ x 13⁸

Gar. 21⁰ x 25⁴

10'-0" CEILING

PANT. R.

D. W.

DN

Br. 2 11⁰ x 13⁰

9'-0" CEILING

Br. 3 12⁰ x 11⁴

10'-0" CEILING

E.

Din. 12⁰ x 15⁴

10'-0" CEILING

Off. 11⁰ x 18⁰ ❶

9'-0" CEILING

COVERED   PORCH

40' - 0"

76' - 8"

© design basics inc.

The dining room has a streamlined path to the kitchen. It's location, however, also makes it useful as a second living area.

Both secondary bedrooms offer tall ceilings and views to the front.

SOLUTION

The Coopers Farm is well suited to the needs of today's work-at-home parent. A large office (❶, at left) is privately located from the living areas of the home. It also features a door to the outside, useful to accommodate client visits. Seclusion is also an asset of the office in the Briarwood (❷, at right plus interior view). Plenty of natural light adorns this working space.

Br. 4
13⁰ x 11⁰

16' – 10" CEILING

OPEN
TO
BELOW

DN

LINEN

PLANT
SHELF

Br. 2
12⁰ x 12⁰

Br. 3
12⁰ x 12⁰

TRANSOMS

Grt. rm.
20⁰ x 16⁰

SLOPED CEILING

Mbr.
14⁰ x 15⁰
12' – 0" CLG.

DRESSER

Bfst.
13⁰ x 12⁰

②

SNACK BAR

Off.
11⁴ x 10⁰
10' – 0" CEILING

TRANSOMS

Kit.
13⁰ x 14⁵

PANT.

D. / W.

FOLDING
TABLE

WHIRLPOOL

11' – 0"
CLG.

SHELF

UP

DN

E.

Din.
15⁰ x 12⁰

HUTCH

Gar.
21⁴ x 32⁰

COVERED
PORCH

© design basics inc.

59' – 4"

60' – 0"

This convenient laundry room provides a folding table, soaking sink and plenty of counter space.

The arrangement of the kitchen counters allows for working space that's handy when serving the dining room.

A built-in dresser saves space in the master bedroom, allowing room for other furniture pieces.

Briarwood

#28B-2956 Price Code B25

Main Floor: 1875 Sq. Ft.
Second Floor: 687 Sq. Ft.
Total Square Feet: 2562 Sq. Ft.

HOME OFFICE . . .

With today's advanced technology, it's not surprising that many professionals bring their work home, or solely work out of their home in order to have more time with their families. Several strategically-planned designs with suitable options for a home office are featured below.

QUIET WORKING SPACE

| Main Floor: 1273 Sq. Ft. |
| Second Floor: 1035 Sq. Ft. |
| Total Square Feet: 2308 Sq. Ft. |

Hartman

#28B-3333 Price Code B23

A grand hutch space is featured in the dining room, perfect for china storage and display in a favored antique.

A large family room that opens to the breakfast area and kitchen provides needed space for family gatherings.

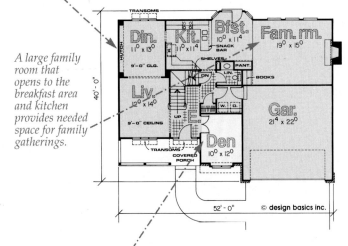

Double doors open to a cozy den located in a quiet area of the home for working privacy.

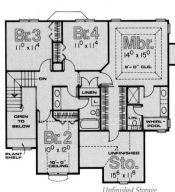

Unfinished Storage Adds 172 Square Feet

PEACEFUL LIBRARY

| Main Floor: 1709 Sq. Ft. |
| Second Floor: 1597 Sq. Ft. |
| Total Square Feet: 3306 Sq. Ft. |

Abbey

#28B-1510 Price Code B33

A large gourmet kitchen, combined with the breakfast area and spacious family room offers amenities such as an island snack bar, fireplace and wet bar.

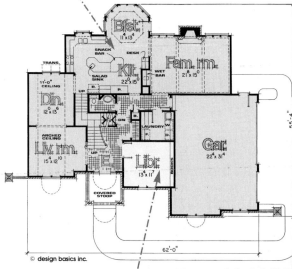

Complete with an ample bookshelf that creates a warm, studious atmosphere, the library offers a quaint place for working out of the home.

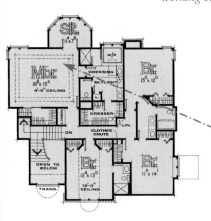

The lavish master suite has a beautiful tiered ceiling, two walk-in closets, built-in dresser and, through double doors, a private gazebo sitting area.

♦ SEASONS OF LIFE ~The SUMMER YEAR

MID-LEVEL DEN

Main Floor: 1583 Sq. Ft.	
Second Floor: 1331 Sq. Ft.	
Total Square Feet: 2914 Sq. Ft.	

Manning

#28B-2207 Price Code B29

The family room, with its striking bowed windows, shares a showy 3-sided fireplace with the kitchen and breakfast area.

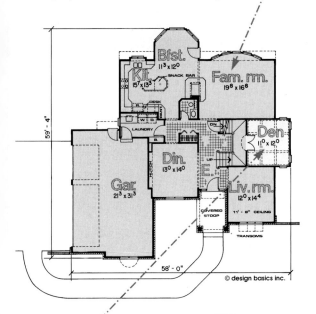

With its spider-beamed ceiling and elegant French doors, the mid-level den offers a private area for work or study.

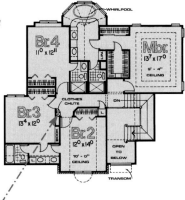

A second-floor clothes chute makes doing laundry convenient for the whole family.

SUNNY HOME STUDY

Main Floor: 1463 Sq. Ft.	
Second Floor: 1385 Sq. Ft.	
Total Square Feet: 2848 Sq. Ft.	

Lynnwood

#28B-3247 Price Code B28

Through an angled entry and double doors is a private den with a beautiful bayed window.

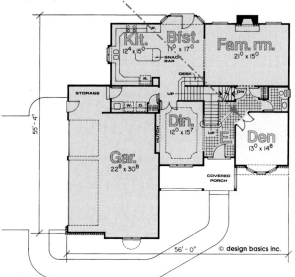

An unfinished bonus room provides options for storage or expansion.

A built-in window seat in bedroom 3 is a great place to read and study.

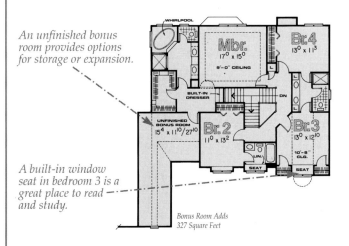

Bonus Room Adds
327 Square Feet

S. Janicek

CONVENIENT COMPUTER CENTER

Collier

Main Floor: 1224 Sq. Ft.
Second Floor: 950 Sq. Ft.
Total Square Feet: 2174 Sq. Ft.

#28B-2216 Price Code B21

Welcome Work Space

Hartley

Main Floor: 1216 Sq. Ft.
Second Floor: 1188 Sq. Ft.
Total Square Feet: 2404 Sq. Ft.

#28B-2949 Price Code B24

For studying or planning, a built-in desk is conveniently located in the kitchen and breakfast area.

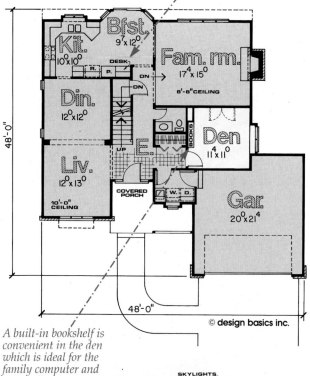

Bfst. 9'x12'
Kit. 10'x10'
Fam. rm. 17'⁴x15'
8'-8" CEILING
DESK
R. P.
DN
DN
Din. 12'x12'
Den 11'⁴x11'
BOOKS
Liv. 12'x13'
10'-0" CEILING
UP
E
COVERED PORCH
W. D.
Gar. 20'x21'⁴
48'-0"
48'-0"

© design basics inc.

A built-in bookshelf is convenient in the den which is ideal for the family computer and home office.

The irresistible master suite includes a whirlpool, skylit vanity and a roomy walk-in closet.

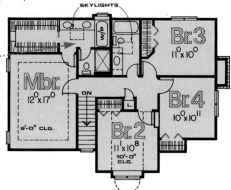

SKYLIGHTS
W/P
Br. 3 11'x10'
Mbr. 12'x17'
9'-0" CLG.
DN
L.
Br. 4 10'x10'¹¹
Br. 2 11'x10'⁸
10'-0" CLG.

French doors lead to a secluded den, perfect for a home office with abundant space for a desk and computer credenza.

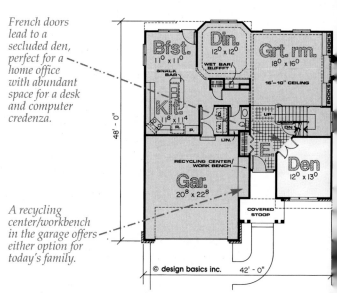

Bfst. 11'x11'
Din. 12'x12'
WET BAR / BUFFET
Grt. rm. 18'x16'
16'-10" CEILING
BOOKS
SNACK BAR
Kit. 11'⁸x11'⁴
R. P.
W.
LIN.
UP
DN
E
RECYCLING CENTER / WORK BENCH
Gar. 20'⁸x22'⁸
Den 12'x13'
COVERED STOOP

© design basics inc. 42'-0" 48'-0"

A recycling center/workbench in the garage offers either option for today's family.

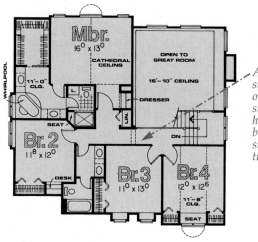

Mbr. 16'x13'
CATHEDRAL CEILING
OPEN TO GREAT ROOM
16'-10" CEILING
WHIRLPOOL
11'-0" CLG.
SEAT
DRESSER
LIN.
DN
Br. 2 11'⁸x12'
DESK
Br. 3 11'x13'
Br. 4 12'x12'⁶
11'-8" CLG.
SEAT

A generous stairway landing overlooks the 2-story great room highlighted by built-in cabinets surrounding a tiled fireplace.

OPTIMAL OFFICE

Main Floor: 1535 Sq. Ft.
Second Floor: 962 Sq. Ft.
Total Square Feet: 2497 Sq. Ft.

Lawler

#28B-2898 Price Code B24

...rsatile main-level office is spacious and private, with its own bath-
... and access to the outside through an attractive covered stoop.

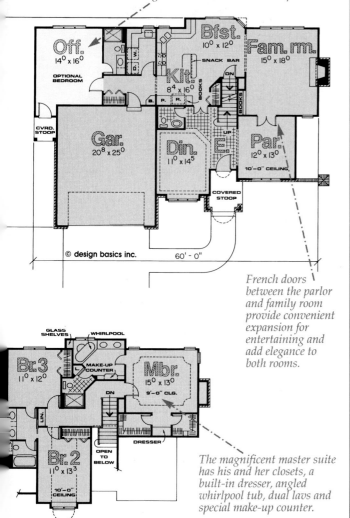

Off. 14⁰ x 16⁰
OPTIONAL BEDROOM
Bfst. 10⁰ x 12⁰
SNACK BAR
Fam. rm. 15⁰ x 18⁰
Kit. 8⁴ x 16⁰
BOOKS
CVRD. STOOP
Gar. 20⁸ x 25⁰
Din. 11⁰ x 14⁵
Par. 12⁰ x 13⁰
10'-0" CEILING
COVERED STOOP
© design basics inc.   60' - 0"

French doors between the parlor and family room provide convenient expansion for entertaining and add elegance to both rooms.

GLASS SHELVES
WHIRLPOOL
Br. 3 11⁰ x 12⁰
MAKE-UP COUNTER
Mbr. 15⁰ x 13⁰
9'-0" CLG.
DN
LIN.
DRESSER
Br. 2 11⁰ x 13³
10'-0" CEILING
OPEN TO BELOW

The magnificent master suite has his and her closets, a built-in dresser, angled whirlpool tub, dual lavs and special make-up counter.

LOGICAL LIBRARY

Main Floor: 1857 Sq. Ft.
Second Floor: 1754 Sq. Ft.
Total Square Feet: 3611 Sq. Ft.

Glencross

#28B-3388 Price Code B36

The stately library is ideal for work or study, and features a large bookcase and double doors.

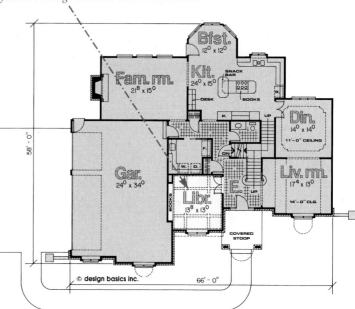

Bfst. 12⁰ x 12⁰
Fam. rm. 21⁸ x 15⁰
Kit. 24⁰ x 15⁰
SNACK BAR
DESK
BOOKS
Din. 14⁰ x 14⁰
11'-0" CEILING
Gar. 24⁰ x 34⁰
W. D.
Libr. 13⁸ x 13⁰
BOOKS
Liv. rm. 17⁴ x 13⁰
14'-0" CLG.
COVERED STOOP
58' - 0"
66' - 0"
© design basics inc.

The exquisite master suite indulges the head of the household with a spacious, sunny sitting area.

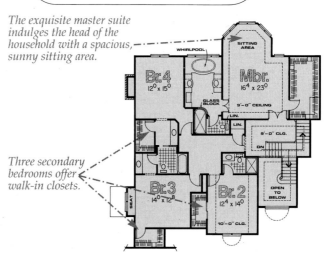

WHIRLPOOL
SITTING AREA
Br. 4 12⁰ x 15⁰
GLASS BLOCK
LIN.
Mbr. 16⁴ x 23⁰
9'-0" CEILING
9'-0" CLG.
DN
Br. 3 14⁰ x 12⁸
SEAT
Br. 2 12⁴ x 14⁰
10'-0" CLG.
OPEN TO BELOW

Three secondary bedrooms offer walk-in closets.

OPEN FAMILY AREAS . . .

Gathering together with friends and family is one of life's greatest joys. But having adequate space to accommodate them can be a challenge. Living and kitchen areas that are connected make entertaining large groups comfortable. Open family areas are key features of these well-planned home designs.

FAVORABLE FAMILY DESIGN

Main Floor:	1122 Sq. Ft.
Second Floor:	1409 Sq. Ft.
Total Square Feet:	2531 Sq. Ft.

Laveen

#28B-5209 Price Code B25

NOTE: 9 ft. main level walls

A generous family room with nearby breakfast area and kitchen provide adequate space for family activities and time together.

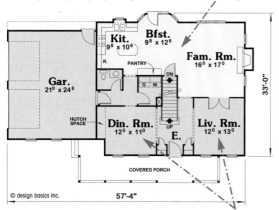

The dining and living rooms have flexible locations and feature hutch space and French doors.

A large master suite is located on the second floor near three large secondary bedrooms, all designed with roomy walk-in closets and ample bathroom arrangements.

FRIENDLY FAMILY ATMOSPHERE

Main Floor:	1057 Sq. Ft.
Second Floor:	869 Sq. Ft.
Total Square Feet:	1926 Sq. Ft.

Oak Hollow

#28B-8081 Price Code A19

The large family room is joined with the breakfast area and kitchen, creating a comfortable area for relaxation.

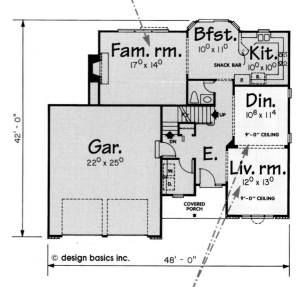

Viewed from the entry, the volume living room and connecting volume dining room provide an open and friendly atmosphere for gatherings and entertaining.

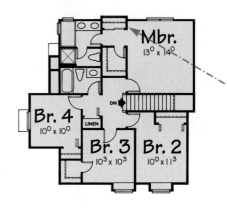

A second closet in the master bedroom provides additional room for clothing and storage.

GREAT GRILLING PORCH

Main Floor: 989 Sq. Ft.	
Second Floor: 1039 Sq. Ft.	
Total Square Feet: 2028 Sq. Ft.	

Ballobin

#28B-3552 Price Code B20

HOLIDAY EXPANSION

Main Floor: 1000 Sq. Ft.	
Second Floor: 1298 Sq. Ft.	
Total Square Feet: 2298 Sq. Ft.	

Millard Oaks

#28B-8024 Price Code A22

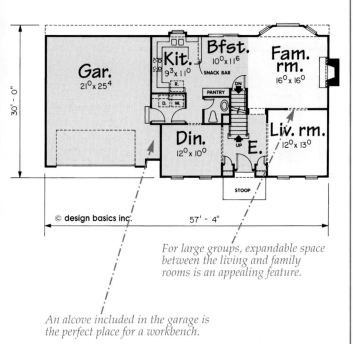

For large groups, expandable space between the living and family rooms is an appealing feature.

An alcove included in the garage is the perfect place for a workbench.

Openness is key in the grand family room with connection to the breakfast area and access to a quaint covered porch.

The dining room is easily useable as a parlor or home office and has a lovely view of the covered front porch.

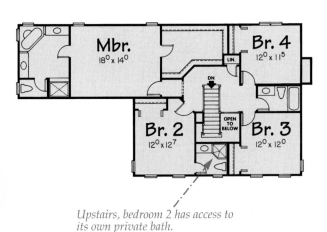

Upstairs, bedroom 2 has access to its own private bath.

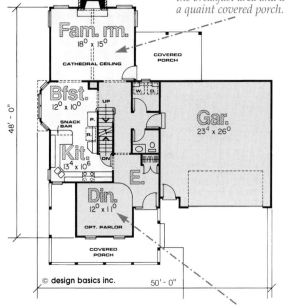

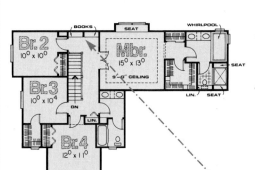

Built-in bookshelves are great places to display family photographs, trophies and memorabilia.

FAMILY ROOM TOGETHERNESS

| Main Floor: 1134 Sq. Ft. |
| Second Floor: 1149 Sq. Ft. |
| Total Square Feet: 2283 Sq. Ft. |

Lindsey

#28B-3376 Price Code B22

French doors open expansively to a warm family room and kitchen area.

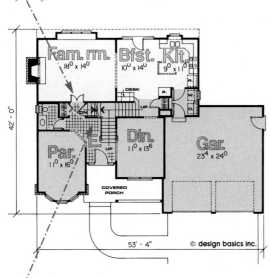

© design basics inc.

A T-shaped stairway keeps the children's traffic from the formal area of the home.

Spaciousness abounds in the master suite's walk-in closet and bath.

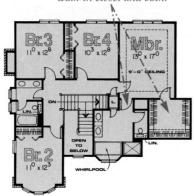

OPEN SNACK SERVICE

| Main Floor: 1000 Sq. Ft. |
| Second Floor: 993 Sq. Ft. |
| Total Square Feet: 1993 Sq. Ft. |

Harrisburg

#28B-2315 Price Code B19

A gourmet kitchen and breakfast area profit from an extra-large pantry, two lazy Susans and a patio door to the rear yard.

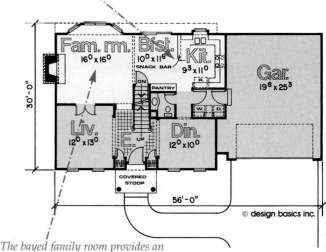

© design basics inc.

The bayed family room provides an ideal area to gather and relax with its raised hearth fireplace and expansion into the living room.

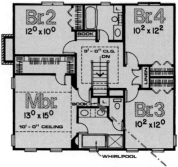

Built-in bookshelves provide a place for family photos and other memorabilia.

Warm Reaching Fireplace

Sherman Oaks

Main Floor: 852 Sq. Ft.
Second Floor: 1029 Sq. Ft.
Total Square Feet: 1881 Sq. Ft.

#28B-8098 Price Code A18

The large family room in this home has a view to the back and a comfortable fireplace.

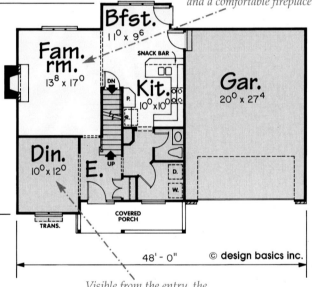

Bfst. 11⁰ x 9⁶
Fam. rm. 13⁸ x 17⁰
SNACK BAR
Kit. 10⁰ x 10⁰
Gar. 20⁰ x 27⁴
Din. 10⁰ x 12⁰
E.
COVERED PORCH
TRANS.
48'- 0"
© design basics inc.

Visible from the entry, the dining room offers flexible options as a den or parlor.

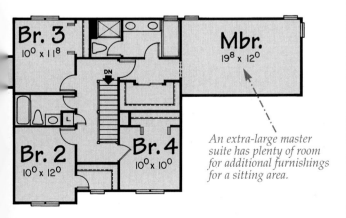

Br. 3 10⁰ x 11⁸
Br. 2 10⁰ x 12⁰
Br. 4 10⁰ x 10⁰
Mbr. 19⁸ x 12⁰

An extra-large master suite has plenty of room for additional furnishings for a sitting area.

Outdoor Eating Porch

Columbus

Main Floor: 941 Sq. Ft.
Second Floor: 992 Sq. Ft.
Total Square Feet: 1933 Sq. Ft.

#28B-2963 Price Code B19

A covered porch can be accessed from the breakfast area, and offers great expansion when entertaining family and friends.

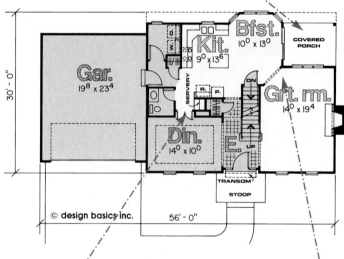

Bfst. 10⁰ x 13⁰
Kit. 9⁰ x 13⁰
COVERED PORCH
Gar. 19⁸ x 23⁴
SERVERY
Grt. rm. 14⁰ x 19⁴
Din. 14⁰ x 10⁰
E.
TRANSOM
STOOP
30'- 0"
56'- 0"
© design basics inc.

Opening conveniently to the kitchen through elegant French doors, the expansive dining room is located just inside the entry.

Adding uniqueness to the home, an angled, cased opening connects the large great room and bayed breakfast area.

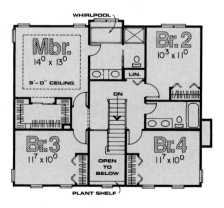

WHIRLPOOL
Mbr. 14⁰ x 13⁰
9'- 0" CEILING
Br. 2 10³ x 11⁰
LIN.
Br. 3 11⁷ x 10⁰
Br. 4 11⁷ x 10⁰
OPEN TO BELOW
PLANT SHELF

To Build Or Not To Build

A home, unlike the four walls-and-a-door make up of a house, takes years of shaping... It takes time to establish memories within it. In other words, its carpet must be spilled upon, its woodwork nicked by the everyday mishaps of our everyday lives.

In the same way that Rome wasn't built in a day, a house doesn't turn into a "home" overnight. A home, unlike the four-walls-and-a-door make up of a house, takes years of shaping. It takes our efforts to form relationships with the neighborhood. It takes time to establish memories within it. In other words, its carpet must be spilled upon, its woodwork nicked by the everyday mishaps of our everyday lives. We have to memorize its patterns. We must be able to walk through it in the dark and know every creak in its floors. It – at the very least – must be the place where we think we are during those first moments of waking up while on vacation. No house is a home overnight. Not even one's dream home.

My dream home is a two-story. It has a flexible den just inside the entry that could just as easily be used as a dining room

Woodvine Manor

#28B-9161 Price Code C27

Main Floor: 1400 Sq. Ft.
Second Floor: 1315 Sq. Ft.
Total Square Feet: 2715 Sq. Ft.

NOTE: 9 ft. main level walls

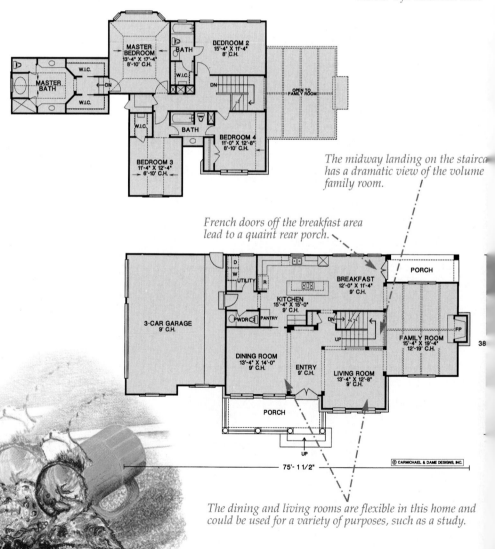

The midway landing on the staircase has a dramatic view of the volume family room.

French doors off the breakfast area lead to a quaint rear porch.

The dining and living rooms are flexible in this home and could be used for a variety of purposes, such as a study.

© CARMICHAEL & DAME DESIGNS, INC.

or bedroom. In general, there are no traditional "formal" rooms within it. It has a large kitchen that is open to an informal eating area and a cozy hearth room. All of its four bedrooms are located on the second floor along with the laundry room. The great room is visible from the entry, but is also a bit secluded, connecting to the kitchen area. Between the kitchen and great room is a rear staircase leading to the second floor. The cedar-shake exterior of the home is reminiscent of traditional Shingle-style architecture, although its overall design is a bit more expansive and less boxy in shape.

I've been considering this dream home of mine lately. My wife and I just recently had our second daughter, and of course that gets one to planning all sorts of grand schemes like saving extra money for her first car and building a dream home that's more suitable to our family's lifestyle.

I think of how much easier it would be to have our bedroom near our girls' bedrooms. Or how that hearth room would be a perfect place to teach my five-year-old how to write her name. I can clearly see us enjoying a football playoff game with friends in the great room and my wife

cont'd on next page

Concorde

#28B-3597 Price Code B21

Total Square Feet: 2132 Sq. Ft.

A secluded family room in this home is warmed by a fireplace between windows.

With three access points, a rear covered patio will be a great place to enjoy the outdoors.

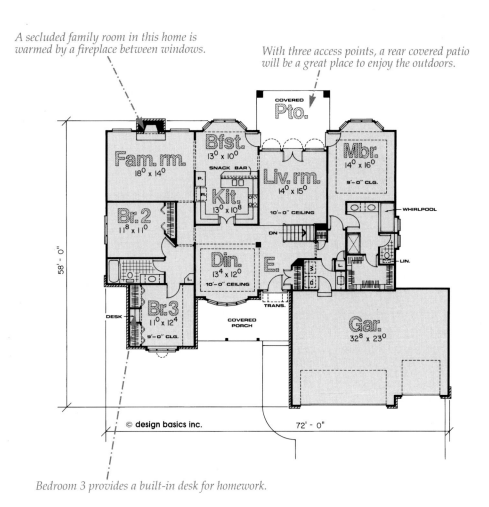

Bedroom 3 provides a built-in desk for homework.

Monterey

#28B-2290 Price Code B16

Total Square Feet: 1666 Sq. Ft.

A rear covered porch makes a great getaway off the breakfast area.

The dining room is expandable in to the great room when serving large groups.

An alcove in the garage would welcome storage shelves.

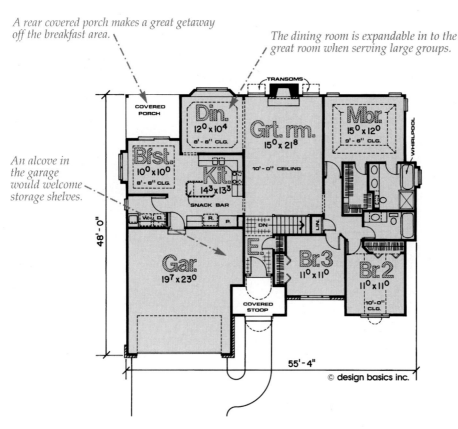

COVERED PORCH

Din.
12⁰ x 10⁴
8' - 8" CLG.

Grt. rm.
15⁰ x 21⁸
10' - 0" CEILING

Mbr.
15⁰ x 12⁰
9' - 8" CLG.

WHIRLPOOL

TRANSOMS

Bfst.
10⁰ x 10⁰
8' - 8" CLG.

Kit.
14³ x 13³

SNACK BAR

W. D.

R.

DN.

LIN.

Gar.
19⁷ x 23⁰

E.

Br. 3
11⁰ x 11⁰

Br. 2
11⁰ x 11⁰
10'-0" CLG.

COVERED STOOP

48' - 0"

55' - 4"

© design basics inc.

I think of how much easier it would be to have our bedroom near our girls' bedrooms. Or how that hearth room would be a perfect place to teach my five-year-old how to write her name. throwing in a load of laundry before she even descends to the main level in the morning. Its Nantucket spirit would emit a sense of warmth and unpretentiousness to all.

Then why don't you build it? says a small voice in my head, responding to these thoughts. I hesitate, because another voice emits an overwhelming sense of uncertainty. Would this dream house "feel" like home? Or would this home that I've imagined for so long be too perfect to relax in? Would its newness force us to put plastic coverings on our furniture and sit up straight with our hands in our laps? Would we start taking our shoes off in the entry so we wouldn't track the outdoors onto its floors? Would my daughters' crayons be forbidden in every area of the home except the kitchen table under close supervision? Would it change me also, so that I would stop telling old stories about my childhood adventures

cont'd on next page

✦ SEASONS OF LIFE ~The Summer Years ✦

Pinehurst

#28B-2311 Price Code B24

Family activity will be held in the seclusion of the unique kitchen, breakfast area and gathering room.

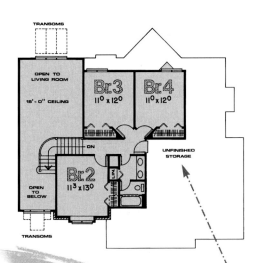

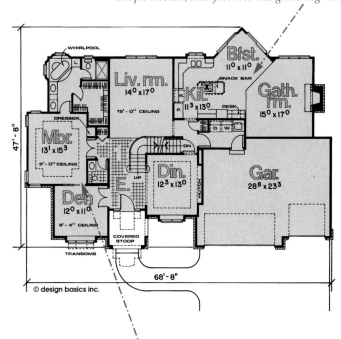

An unfinished area above the garage would make great additional space for storage.

A pocket door connects the master suite and den.

Main Floor: 1829 Sq. Ft.
Second Floor: 657 Sq. Ft.
Total Square Feet: 2486 Sq. Ft.

Bancroft

#28B-1559 Price Code B18

Total Square Feet: 1808 Sq. Ft.

A wet bar is conveniently located between the great room and breakfast area.

Work shelves can be built in a storage area available in the garage.

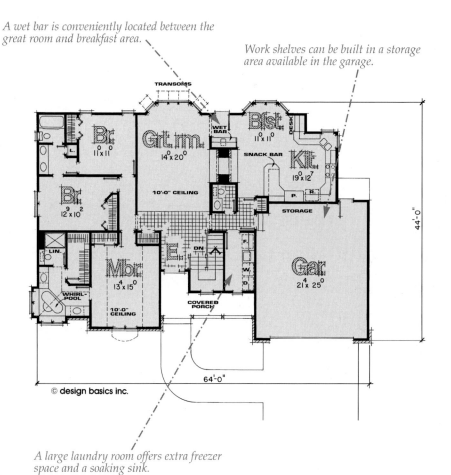

© design basics inc.

A large laundry room offers extra freezer space and a soaking sink.

in favor of discussing the latest merger on Wall Street?

Then don't build your dream home at all, says the same voice in my head. Don't build my dream home? But it's perfect for my family, I say to myself. If there ever was a home for us, it's this home, I acknowledge. It has gradually formed its simplistic, clean facade in my head. In fact, it practically designed itself with our every nonchalant "wouldn't-it-be-nice-to-have" comment. In my head, I know all of my new neighbors. Its atmosphere has lulled my children to sleep. For the many times I've imagined it, I've practically lived in it for years.

Considering the conviction of my thoughts, the small voice in my head quickly quiets. Through simply questioning my doubtfulness, the voice reveals the wisdom of what I have known all along. As much as a home is a physical place, it is a psychological decision one makes about where they live. And in my case, I've already decided where my home is. Of course I will build it. ◆

Would its newness force us to put plastic coverings on our furniture and sit up straight... Would we start taking our shoes off in the entry so we wouldn't track the outdoors onto its floors?

Dundee

#28B-2476 Price Code B28

Main Floor: 2183 Sq. Ft.
Second Floor: 701 Sq. Ft.
Total Square Feet: 2884 Sq. Ft.

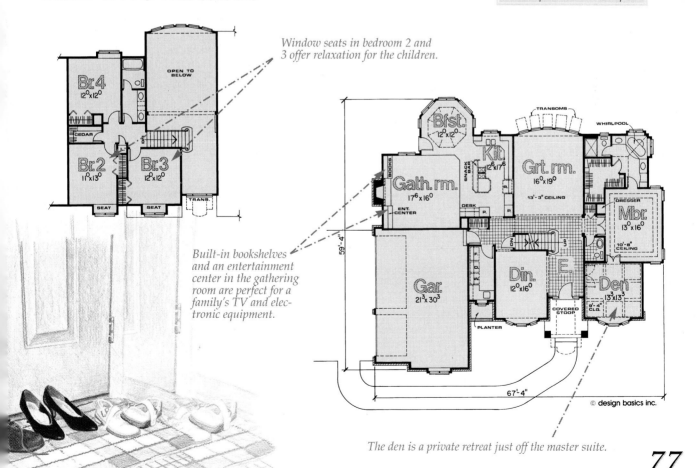

Window seats in bedroom 2 and 3 offer relaxation for the children.

Built-in bookshelves and an entertainment center in the gathering room are perfect for a family's TV and electronic equipment.

The den is a private retreat just off the master suite.

Br 4 12⁰x12⁰

OPEN TO BELOW

CEDAR

Br 2 11⁰x13⁰

Br 3 12⁰x12⁰

SEAT   SEAT   TRANS.

Bfst. 12⁰x12⁰

Kit. 12⁰x17⁶

Grt. rm. 16⁰x19⁰
13'-3" CEILING

TRANSOMS

WHIRLPOOL

Gath. rm. 17⁶x16⁰

SNACK BAR

ENT. CENTER

DESK

BOOKS

Mbr. 13⁰x16⁰
10'-8" CEILING

DRESSER

Gar. 21³x30³

Din. 12⁰x16⁰

Den 13³x13³

COVERED STOOP

PLANTER

59'-4"

67'-4"

© design basics inc.

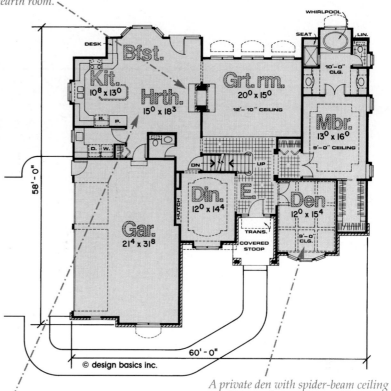

A see-thru fireplace warms both the great room and hearth room.

Functioning as one large living area, the kitchen, hearth room and breakfast area form a central hub for daily activity.

A private den with spider-beam ceiling would be perfect as a home office.

Main Floor: 1972 Sq. Ft.
Second Floor: 673 Sq. Ft.
Total Square Feet: 2645 Sq. Ft.

Armburst

#28B-2723 Price Code B26

FAR LEFT: A decorative ceiling sets the tone in this impressive master suite with French doors leading to the master bath.

LEFT: His and her vanities and compartmented stool and shower show off the whirlpool tub under an arched window.

RIGHT: An elegant staircase makes a beautiful vista between the great room and dining room.

BUILT BY: DOUGLAS YOUNG BUILDER
PHOTOS BY: TOM WEIGAND

The home in these photographs may be altered from the original plan.

SITUATION

One of my biggest pet peeves about our current home is its lack of storage space. We live in an area without basements, and frankly, I'm tired of cramming boxes into my bedroom closet and my children's tiny closets that were meant to only hang clothing. In our next home, it's extremely important that we have larger bedroom closets and a place to put our Christmas decorations, memorabilia and the other "stuff" that we've accumulated over the years . . .

SOLUTION

The Schuyler (❶, at far right), not only offers a large storage area on the second floor, it also offers the potential for extra storage in a walk-in closet located in bedroom 2. In the Autumn Hills (❷, at right), a bonus room is located on the second floor along with three secondary bedrooms. It offers more than enough storage space to accommodate this four-bedroom household.

Autumn Hills

#28B-8055 Price Code A23

Main Floor: 1620 Sq. Ft.
Second Floor: 702 Sq. Ft.
Total Square Feet: 2322 Sq. Ft.

Br. 3 11⁰ x 13⁰
Br. 4 10⁸ x 13⁰
Br. 2 12⁰ x 13⁷
10'-0" CEILING
OPEN TO BELOW
PLANT SHELF
DN
L
L
Bonus ❷ UNFINISHED 20⁸ x 21⁴

Unfinished Bonus Room Adds 325 Square Feet

A see-thru fireplace warms both the breakfast area and great room.

This large laundry room is equipped with a soaking sink and extra counter space for folding clothes.

TRANSOMS
Grt. rm. 16⁰ x 20⁰ 17'-0" CEILING
Bfst. 14³ x 15⁰
Kit. 10⁰ x 13⁰
Mbr. 13⁰ x 17⁰ 10'-0" CLG.
E.
Din. 12⁰ x 14⁰
Gar. 31⁴ x 22⁰
UP
DN
P.
R.
D. W.
COVERED STOOP
48'-8"
65'-4"
© design basics inc.

The large master suite includes a soaking tub, volume ceiling and room for chairs to create a private area by the window.

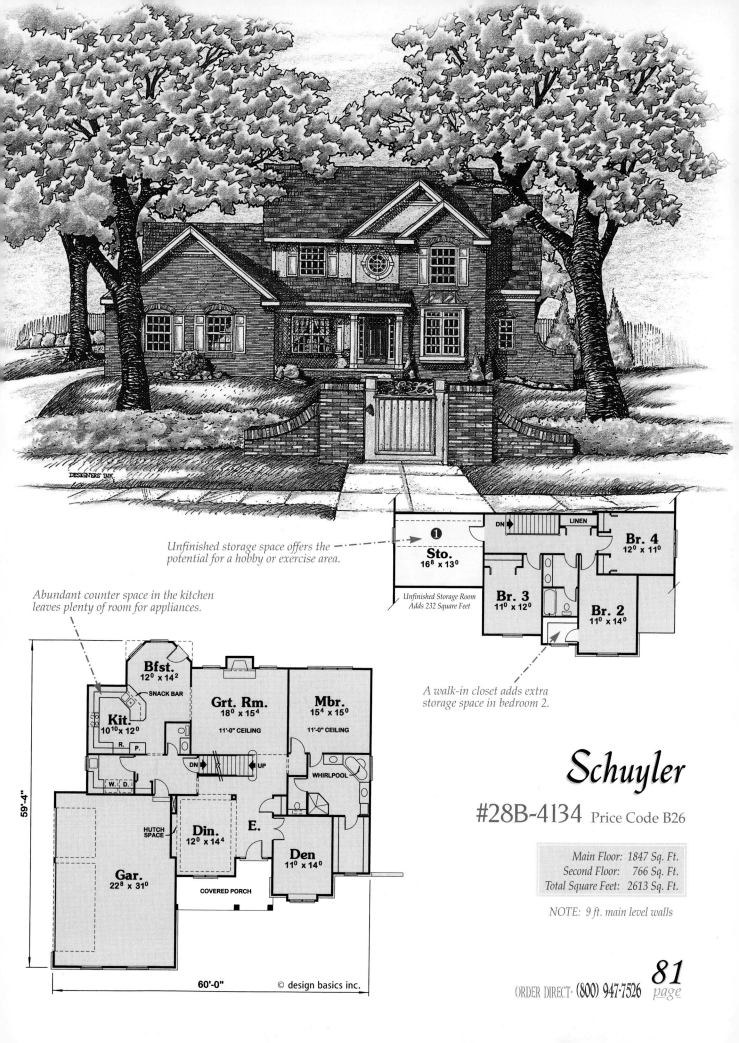

Unfinished storage space offers the potential for a hobby or exercise area.

①

Sto.
16⁸ x 13⁰

DN

LINEN

Br. 4
12⁰ x 11⁰

Br. 3
11⁰ x 12⁰

Br. 2
11⁰ x 14⁰

Unfinished Storage Room Adds 232 Square Feet

Abundant counter space in the kitchen leaves plenty of room for appliances.

A walk-in closet adds extra storage space in bedroom 2.

Bfst.
12⁰ x 14²

SNACK BAR

Grt. Rm.
18⁰ x 15⁴
11'-0" CEILING

Mbr.
15⁴ x 15⁰
11'-0" CEILING

Kit.
10¹⁰ x 12⁰

R.   P.

DN   UP

WHIRLPOOL

W.   D.

59'-4"

HUTCH SPACE

Din.
12⁰ x 14⁴

E.

Den
11⁰ x 14⁰

Gar.
22⁸ x 31⁰

COVERED PORCH

60'-0"

© design basics inc.

Schuyler

#28B-4134 Price Code B26

Main Floor:	1847 Sq. Ft.
Second Floor:	766 Sq. Ft.
Total Square Feet:	2613 Sq. Ft.

NOTE: 9 ft. main level walls

DESIGNERS' INK.

ORDER DIRECT· (800) 947-7526

SITUATION

The name of the game for our family is convenience. The more practical and easy-to-use, the better suited to our lifestyle. One of the most impractical areas of our home is the laundry room. Its location is far away from where most of the laundry is generated in our home — the bedrooms. I'd rather not have to carry laundry baskets back and forth from the kid's rooms. It would make more sense if our laundry room was located near the bedrooms. . .

SOLUTION

The laundry room location in the Cameron (❶, at far right), reduces a family's room-to-room traffic. Featuring its own closet, this laundry room is ideally suited to serve the secondary bedrooms. The Linden Acres showcases the laundry room on the second floor (❷, at right). Because of this, all second-floor bedrooms have easy access to its soaking sink and built-in rod to hang dry clothing.

Linden Acres

#28B-8029 Price Code A17

His and her walk-in closets are an added benefit to the master suite.

Br. 2 10⁰ x 11⁰

Mbr. 13⁰ x 15⁰

Br. 3 10¹¹ x 10⁰

A staircase located towards the back of the home cuts down on traffic in the entry.

Bfst. 10⁰ x 10⁰

SNACK BAR

Grt. rm. 17⁸ x 14⁰

Kit. 10⁰ x 11¹⁰

Din. 13³ x 12⁴

E.

Gar. 19⁴ x 25⁴

COVERED PORCH

40' - 0"

© design basics inc. 44' - 8"

Main Floor: 860 Sq. Ft.
Second Floor: 893 Sq. Ft.
Total Square Feet: 1753 Sq. Ft.

The bayed dining room is within steps of the kitchen and could also serve as a second living area.

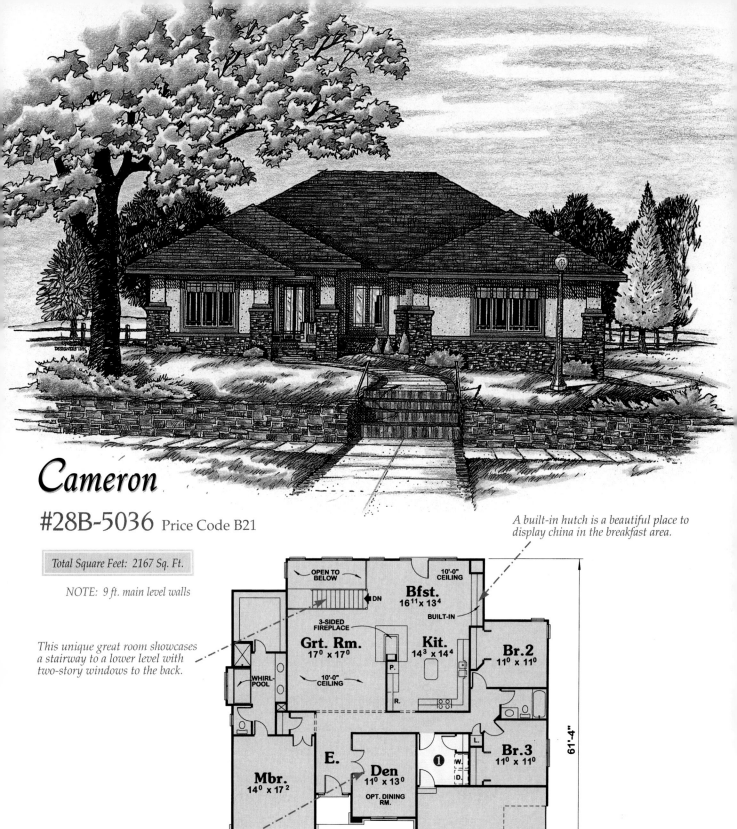

Cameron

#28B-5036 Price Code B21

Total Square Feet: 2167 Sq. Ft.

NOTE: 9 ft. main level walls

A built-in hutch is a beautiful place to display china in the breakfast area.

This unique great room showcases a stairway to a lower level with two-story windows to the back.

Double doors lead to a den which could also be adapted to become a dining room, depending on a family's lifestyle.

OPEN TO BELOW

DN

10'-0" CEILING

Bfst.
16¹¹ x 13⁴

BUILT-IN

3-SIDED FIREPLACE

Grt. Rm.
17⁰ x 17⁰

10'-0" CEILING

Kit.
14³ x 14⁴

Br.2
11⁰ x 11⁰

WHIRL-POOL

P.

R.

Mbr.
14⁰ x 17²

E.

Den
11⁰ x 13⁰

OPT. DINING RM.

❶

W.
D.

L.

Br.3
11⁰ x 11⁰

Gar.
22⁸ x 22⁴

61'-4"

© design basics inc.

55'-4"

COPYRIGHT
Cans & Cannots

ALL DESIGN BASICS PLANS HAVE BEEN REGISTERED
WITH THE U.S. COPYRIGHT OFFICE
ORIGINAL
C
DRAFT

These days, it seems almost everybody has a question about what can or cannot be done with copyrighted home plans. At Design Basics, we know US copyright law can sometimes get complex and confusing, but here are a few of the basic points of the law you'll want to remember.

Once you've purchased a plan from us and have received a Design Basics construction license,

You Can . . .

■ Construct the plan as originally designed, or change it to meet your specific needs.
■ Build it as many times as you wish *without* additional reuse fees.
■ Make duplicate blueprint copies as needed for construction.

You Cannot . . .

■ Build our plans without a Design Basics construction license.
■ Copy *any* part of our original designs to create another design of your own.
■ Claim copyright on changes you make to our plans.
■ Give a plan to someone else for construction purposes.
■ Sell the plan.

PROTECT YOUR RIGHTS

to build, modify and reproduce our home plans with a Design Basics construction license.

CONSTRUCTION LICENS

as original purchaser of plan number

is hereby granted a non-transferable, non-exclusive license to build the home depicted in this plan and is given the right to reproduce this plan only as required for such construction. No re-use fee is required if the original purchaser builds this home more than once. Permission is also given to make modifications to this plan, but no permission is given to claim copyright on the original or any derivative works of this plan. No other rights are granted and any further distribution is strictly prohibited.

Signed
Date
License Number

RETAIN IN YOUR FILES
FOR FUTURE REFERENCE

Valid when the
official Gold Seal™
is embossed above.

11112 John Galt Boulevard   Omaha, Nebraska 68137
Toll Free 800-247-PLAN
402-331-9223   FAX 402-331-5507

design basics inc.
HOME PLAN DESIGN SERVICE

CUSTOMIZED PLAN CHANGES

PRICE SCHEDULE

2 X 6 EXTERIOR WALLS .... $150 .....
FROM STANDARD 2 X 4 TO 2 X 6 EXTERIOR WALLS

EACH GARAGE ALTERATION .... $275 .....
- FRONT-ENTRY TO SIDE LOAD (OR VICE VERSA)
- 2-CAR TO 3-CAR (OR VICE VERSA)
- 2-CAR FRONT-ENTRY TO 3-CAR SIDE -LOAD (OR VICE VERSA)
- 3-CAR FRONT-ENTRY TO 2-CAR SIDE -LOAD (OR VICE VERSA)

WALK-OUT BASEMENT.. $175 .....

CRAWL SPACE FOUNDATION .... $225 .....

SLAB FOUNDATION .... $225 .....

STRETCH CHANGES .... $5 per lineal foot of cut

ADDITIONAL BRICK TO SIDES & REAR .... $325 .....

ADDITIONAL BRICK TO FRONT,
   SIDES AND REAR .... $425 .....

ALTERNATE PRELIMINARY ELEVATION .... $150 .....

9-FOOT MAIN LEVEL WALLS.............................. starting at $150

SPECIFY WINDOW BRAND .... $95 .....

POURED CONCRETE FOUNDATION .... $25 .....
   ONLY WITH OTHER CHANGES

ADDING ONE COURSE (8") TO THE FOUNDATION HEIGHT
   ONLY WITH OTHER CHANGES .... $25 .....

NOTE ....
- All plan changes come to you on erasable, reproducible vellums.
- An unchanged set of original vellums is available for only $50 along with your plan changes.
- Design Basics changes are not made to the artist's renderings, electrical, sections or cabinets.
- Prices are subject to change.

ALL PLANS
Customizable

As a part of our commitment to help you achieve the "perfect" home, we offer an extensive variety of plan changes for any Design Basics plan. For those whose decision to purchase a home plan is contingent upon the feasibility of a plan change, our Customer Support Specialists will, in most cases, be able to provide a FREE price quote for the changes.

call us toll-free at

(800) 947-7526

to order plan changes listed here, or if you have questions regarding plan changes not listed.

For many home buyers, visualizing the finished home is a challenge. Our **Study Print & Furniture Layout Guide™** makes it easy. First, the Study Print provides views of all exterior elevations. Secondly, the Furniture Layout Guide provides a "Feel" for room sizes, with a 1/4" scale floor plan, over 100 reusable furniture pieces and helpful tips on space planning. Available for any Design Basics plan.

STUDY PRINT & FURNITURE LAYOUT GUIDE
— $29.95 —